BASICS OF KEYBOARD THEORY

LEVEL 9

Fourth Edition

Julie McIntosh Johnson

J. Johnson Music Publications

5062 Siesta Lane
Yorba Linda, CA 92886
Phone: (714) 961-0257
Fax: (714) 242-9350
www.bktmusic.com
info@bktmusic.com

Basics of Keyboard Theory, Level 9, Fourth Edition

Published by:

J. Johnson Music Publications
5062 Siesta Lane
Yorba Linda, CA 92886 U.S.A.
(714) 961-0257
www.bktmusic.com

©2007 by Julie McIntosh Johnson. Revised.
Previous editions ©1983, 1993, 1997, Julie McIntosh Johnson.
Printed in United States of America

Library of Congress Cataloging in Publication Data

Johnson, Julie Anne McIntosh
Basics of Keyboard Theory, Level 9, Fourth Edition

ISBN 10: 1-891757-09-1
ISBN 13: 978-1-891757-09-9

LC TX 4-721-491

TO THE TEACHER

Intended as a supplement to private or group music lessons, *Basics of Keyboard Theory, Level 9* presents basic theory concepts to the advanced music student. This level is to be used with the student who has had approximately 9-10 years of music lessons, and is playing piano literature at the level of Mozart's Piano Sonatas, or Chopin's Waltzes. The contents of this book correspond with the requirements for Level 9 of the Music Teachers' Association of California *Certificate of Merit™ Piano Syllabus.**

   Basics of Keyboard Theory, Level 9 is divided into twenty-three lessons, with two reviews, and a test at the end. Application of each theory concept is made to piano music of the student's level. Lessons may be combined with one another, or divided in smaller sections, depending on the ability of the student. Whenever possible, it is helpful to demonstrate theory concepts on the keyboard, and apply them to the music the student is playing.

   Learning music theory can be a very rewarding experience for the student when carefully applied to lessons. *Basics of Keyboard Theory, Level 9,* is an important part of learning this valuable subject.

*Certificate of Merit™ is an evaluation program of the Music Teachers' Association of California. Reference to 'Certificate of Merit™' (CM) does not imply endorsement by MTAC of this product.

BASICS OF KEYBOARD THEORY
COMPUTER ACTIVITIES
by
Nancy Plourde
with
Julie McIntosh Johnson and Anita Yee Belansky

Colorful, exciting games that reinforce Basics of Keyboard Theory lessons!

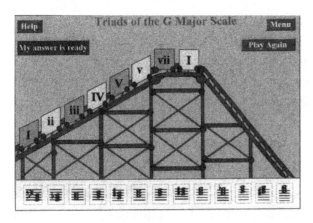

LEVELS PREPARATORY, 1, and 2: 30 GAMES, 10 PER LEVEL!
LEVELS 3 and 4: 20 GAMES, 10 PER LEVEL!
LEVELS 5 and 6: 20 GAMES, 10 PER LEVEL!
Corresponds with MTAC CM Syllabus & *Basics of Keyboard Theory* books, or may be used independently.

Download a free demo at www.pbjmusic.com

--**Order Form**--

Name_____
Address_____
City_____State_____Zip_____
Email_____Phone_____

Mail to: PBJ Music Publications
5062 Siesta Ln.
Yorba Linda, CA 92886
(714) 961-0257

Qty		Cost
_____	Levels Prep-II, Mac/PC: $49.95	_____
_____	Levels III-IV, Mac/PC: $39.95	_____
_____	Levels 5-6, PC only: $49.95	_____
	Sub Total:	_____
	Sales Tax (CA, AZ, TX residents)	_____
	Shipping:	$5.00
	Total:	_____

System Requirements
IBM or compatible: 486 33 MHz or higher, Windows 3.1, 95, 98, NT, XP, or Vista, 8 MB RAM, 5 MB hard disk space, MIDI Soundcard, VGA monitor.
Mac: System 7 or greater, 8 MB RAM, 3 MB hard disk space, color monitor. OS X requires Classic Mode or Boot Camp.

TABLE OF CONTENTS

Basics of Keyboard Theory is dedicated to my husband Rob,
without whose love, support, help, and incredible patience,
this series would not have been possible.

LESSON 1
MAJOR AND MINOR KEY SIGNATURES

The **KEY SIGNATURE** for a musical composition is found at the beginning of the piece, next to the clef signs.

The **KEY SIGNATURE** tells you two things:

1. The **key** or **tonality** of the music.

2. Which notes in the music are to receive sharps or flats.

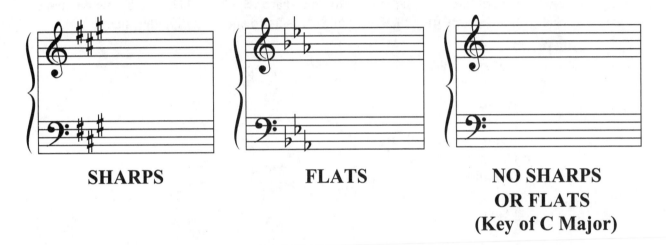

SHARPS   **FLATS**   **NO SHARPS**
OR FLATS
(Key of C Major)

If the key signature has <u>SHARPS</u>, they will be written in this order, on these lines and spaces. This is called the **ORDER OF SHARPS**.

FCGDAEB

THE ORDER OF SHARPS

A saying to help you remember this order is:

Fat Cats Go Down Alleys Eating Bologna

If a key signature has one sharp, it will be F♯. If a key signature has two sharps, they will be F♯ and C♯, etc.

To determine which Major key a group of sharps represents, find and name the last sharp (the sharp furthest to the right), then go up a half step from that sharp. The note which is a half step above the last sharp is the name of the Major key.

Three sharps: F♯, C♯, G♯

Last sharp is G♯

A half step above G♯ is A

Key of A Major

To determine which sharps are in a Major key, find the sharp which is a half step below the name of the key. Name all the sharps from the Order of Sharps up to and including that sharp.

Key of D Major

A half step below D is C♯

Name all sharps, from the Order of Sharps, up to and including C♯

F♯ and C♯

If a key signature has <u>FLATS</u>, they will be in the following order, written on these lines and spaces. This is called the **<u>ORDER OF FLATS.</u>**

BEADGCF

THE ORDER OF FLATS

The Order of Flats can be memorized this way:

BEAD Gum Candy Fruit

If a key signature has one flat, it will be B♭. If it has two flats, they will be B♭ and E♭, etc.

To determine which Major key a group of flats represents, name the next to last flat.

Three flats: B♭, E♭, A♭

Next to last flat is E♭

Key of E♭ Major

To determine which flats are needed for a given key, name all the flats from the Order of Flats up to and including the name of the key, then add one more.

Key of E♭ Major

Name all flats from the Order of Flats up to and including E♭, then add one more.

B♭, E♭, A♭

The key signature for F Major has to be memorized. It has one flat: B♭.

KEY SIGNATURE FOR F MAJOR

Major keys which have sharps will be named with a letter only, or a letter and a sharp (for example, G Major, D Major, F♯ Major).

Major keys which have flats will have a flat in their name (for example, B♭ Major, D♭ Major, E♭ Major).

The two exceptions to the above rules are F Major (one flat: B♭), and C Major (no sharps or flats).

4

1. Name these Major keys.

_____ _____ _____ _____ _____

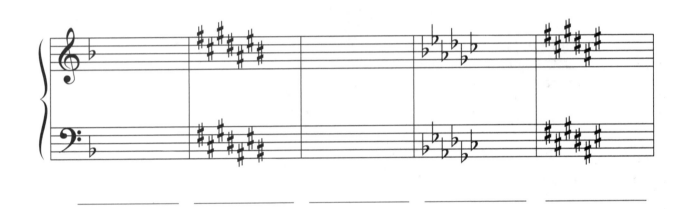

_____ _____ _____ _____ _____

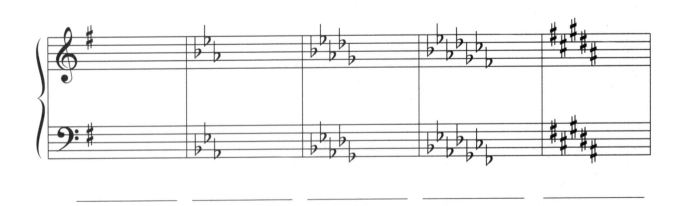

_____ _____ _____ _____ _____

2. Write the key signatures for these Major keys.

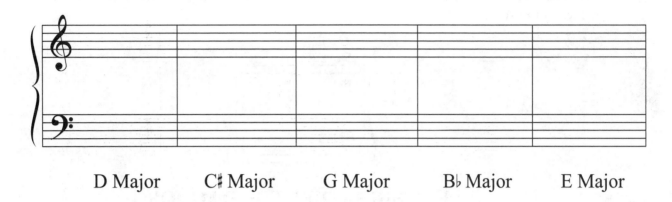

| D Major | C♯ Major | G Major | B♭ Major | E Major |

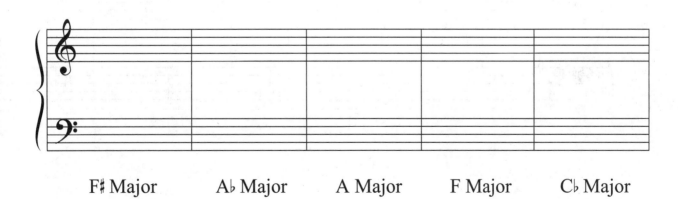

| C Major | B Major | D♭ Major | E♭ Major | G♭ Major |

| F♯ Major | A♭ Major | A Major | F Major | C♭ Major |

6

Many Major key signatures have **RELATIVE MINORS**. The relative minor is found by going down three half steps from the name of the Major key. Skip one letter between the names of the keys.

KEY SIGNATURE FOR D MAJOR
THREE HALF STEPS BELOW D IS B
KEY OF B MINOR

One way to determine whether a composition is in the Major or minor key is to look at the last note of the piece. It is usually the same as the name of the key. (For example, a piece which is in the key of e minor will probably end on E.) Also, look at the music to find the note around which the music appears to be centered. This should be the same as the name of the key.

3. Name these <u>minor</u> keys.

_____ _____ _____ _____ _____ _____

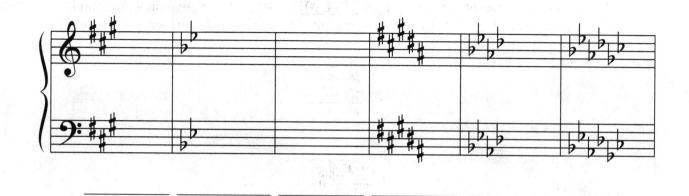

4. Write the key signatures for these minor keys.

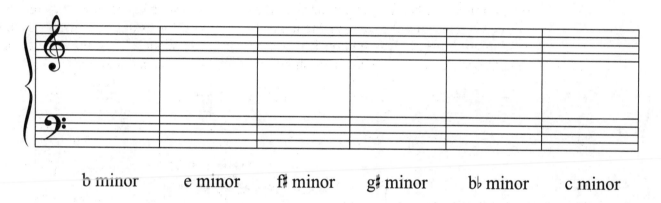

b minor   e minor   f♯ minor   g♯ minor   b♭ minor   c minor

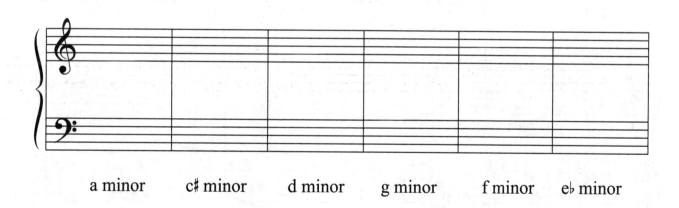

a minor   c♯ minor   d minor   g minor   f minor   e♭ minor

8

5. Give the name of the Major or minor key for each of the following musical examples.

a. From *Invention No. 14* by J.S. Bach. _____

b. From *Sonata, Op. 14, No. 1* by Beethoven. _____

c. From *Nocturne, Op. posth. 72, No. 1,* by Chopin. _____

d. From *Rhapsody, Op. 119, No. 4,* by Brahms. _____

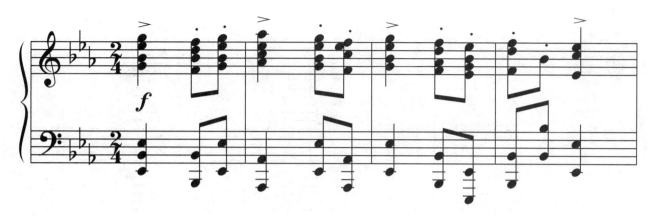

e. From *Sonata, Hob. XVI:19,* by Haydn. _____

f. From *Sinfonia No. 9* by J.S. Bach. _____

g. From *Sonata No. 31* by Scarlatti. _____

h. From *Sonata, Op. 10, No. 1,* by Beethoven. _____

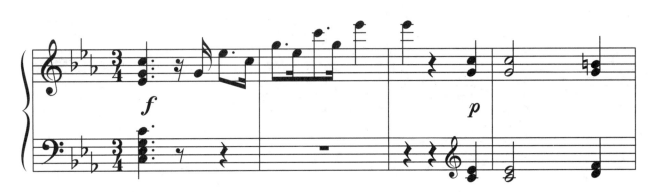

i. From *Waltz, Op. 3, No. 3,* by Britten. _____

The **CIRCLE OF FIFTHS** (sometimes called the **Circle of Keys**) is a method of organizing the Major and minor keys so that when ascending by perfect fifths from key to key, one sharp is added to each new key. When the keys of B, F♯, and C♯ are reached, there is an enharmonic change (notes with the same pitch but different letter names, such as F♯ and G♭). Flats are then used, and as the keys ascend by perfect fifths, one flat is deleted from each key.

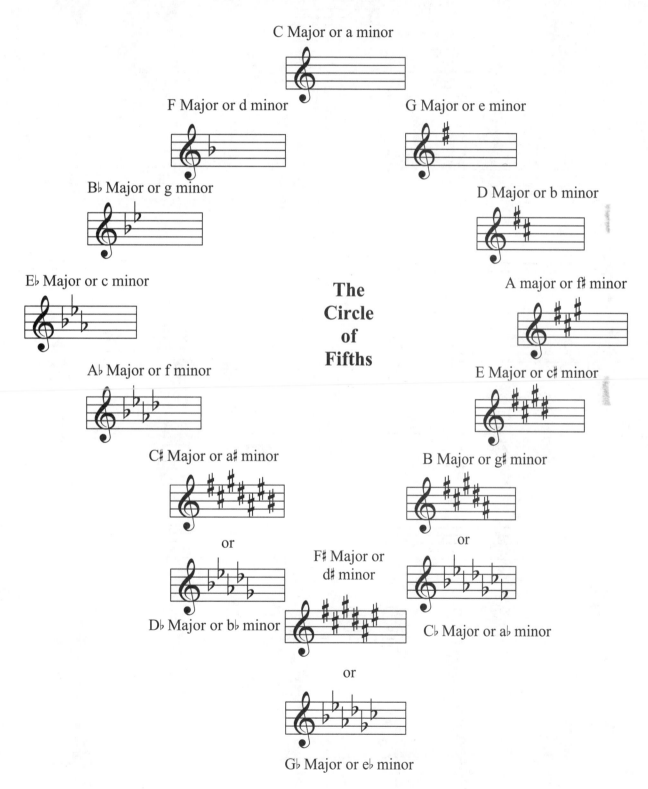

6. Fill in the Circle of Fifths (Circle of Keys) below. Include the Major and minor key names, enharmonic equivalents, and write each key signature on its staff.

The
Circle
of
Fifths

or

or

or

LESSON 2
SCALES AND MODES

__SCALES__ are a series of notes, which are each a step apart. They begin and end with notes of the same letter name.

__MAJOR SCALES__ contain eight notes, and have all the sharps or flats from the Major key signature with the same name. __IONIAN MODE__ has the same pattern of whole and half steps as the major scale.

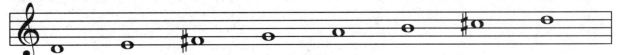

D MAJOR SCALE or IONIAN MODE

__NATURAL MINOR SCALES__ contain all the sharps or flats from the minor key signature with the same name.   Example:d natural minor scale begins and ends with the note "D," and has B♭. __AEOLIAN MODE__ has the same pattern of whole and half steps as the natural minor scale.

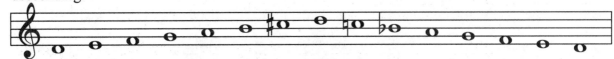

D NATURAL MINOR SCALE or AEOLIAN MODE

__HARMONIC MINOR SCALES__ are created by raising the seventh note of the natural minor scale a half step. This creates a half step, rather than a whole step, between the seventh and eighth notes of the scale, making the seventh a "leading tone."

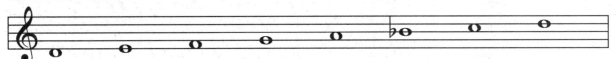

D HARMONIC MINOR SCALE

__MELODIC MINOR SCALES__ are created by raising the sixth and seventh notes of the natural minor scale while ascending, and returning them to natural minor (lowering them) while descending.

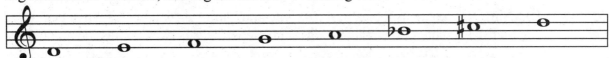

D MELODIC MINOR SCALE

The __CHROMATIC SCALE__ is a series of thirteen notes. Each note is a half step away from its neighbor. Using sharps while the scale is ascending and flats while the scale is descending helps avoid the use of many naturals.

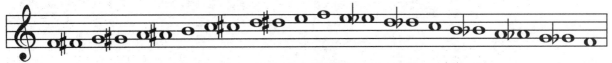

CHROMATIC SCALE BEGINNING ON F

14

The **WHOLE TONE SCALE** consists entirely of whole steps. There are only seven notes in the whole tone scale, so when writing the scale on the staff, one letter name will be missing.

WHOLE TONE SCALE BEGINNING ON D

DORAN MODE contains the pattern of whole and half steps that occurs when beginning and ending on the SECOND note of the major scale. Half steps occur between notes 2-3 and 6-7.

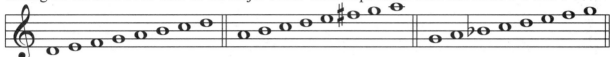

DORIAN MODE

PHRYGIAN MODE contains the pattern of whole and half steps that occurs when beginning and ending on theTHIRD note of the major scale. Half steps occur between notes 1-2 and 5-6.

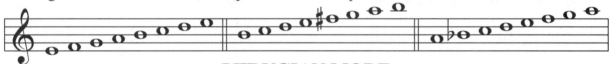

PHRYGIAN MODE

LYDIAN MODE contains the pattern of whole and half steps that occurs when beginning and ending on the FOURTH note of the major scale. Half steps occur between notes 4-5 and 7-8.

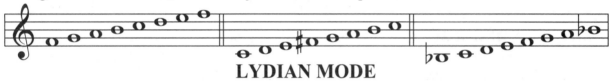

LYDIAN MODE

MIXOLYDIAN MODE contains the pattern of whole and half steps that occurs when beginning and ending on theFIFTH note of the major scale. Half steps occur between notes 3-4 and 6-7

MIXOLYDIAN MODE

AEOLIAN MODE contains the pattern of whole and half steps that occurs when beginning and ending on theSIXTH note of the major scale. Half steps occur between notes 2-3 and 5-6

AEOLIAN MODE

LOCRIAN MODE contains the pattern of whole and half steps that occurs when beginning and ending on theSEVENTH note of the major scale. Half steps occur between notes 1-2 and 4-5.

LOCRIAN MODE

1. Write these scales.

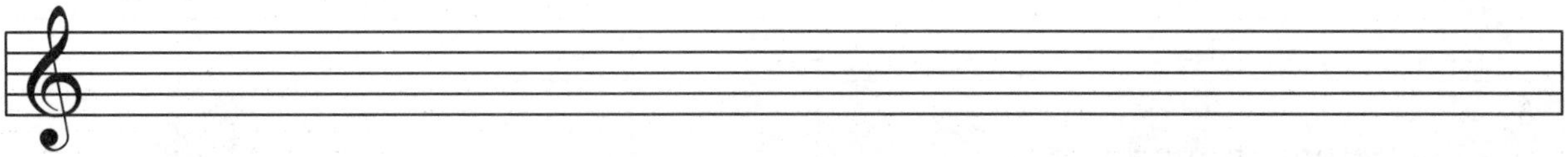

C♯ Major

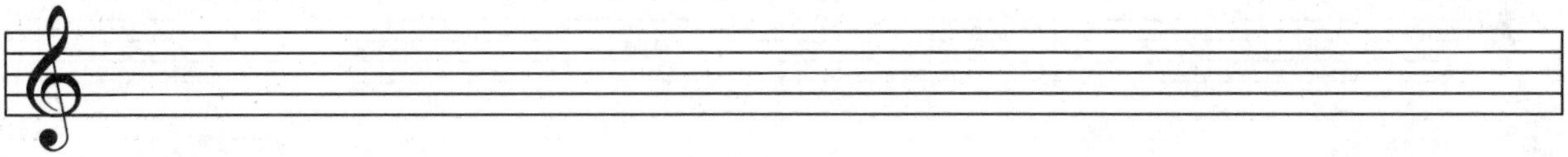

b natural minor

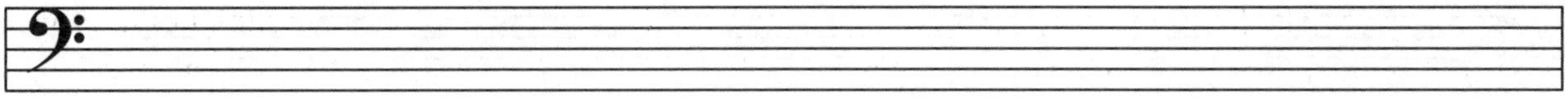

Chromatic beginning on B (ascending and descending)

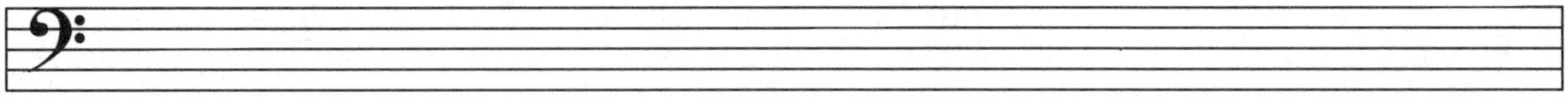

f harmonic minor

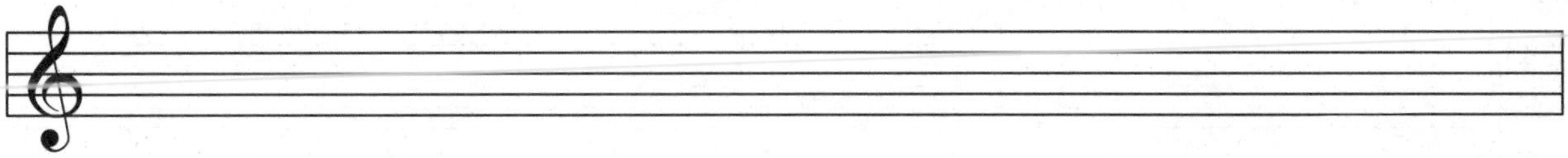

D♭ Major

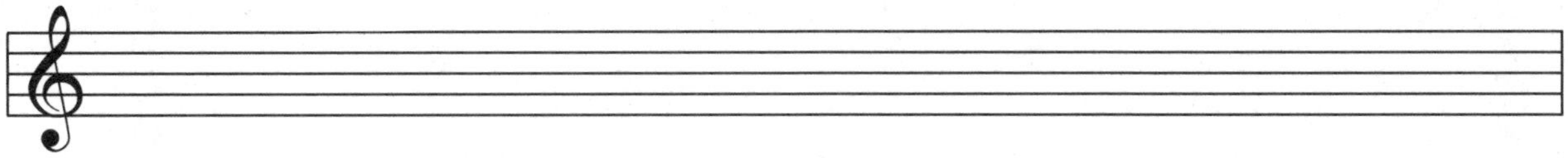

Whole Tone beginning on E

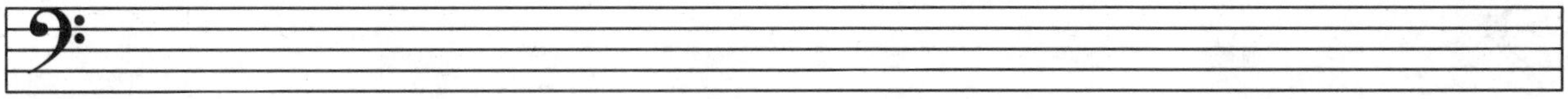

Locrian Mode on E

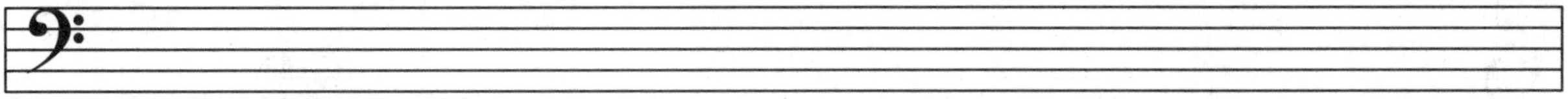

Phrygian Mode on B

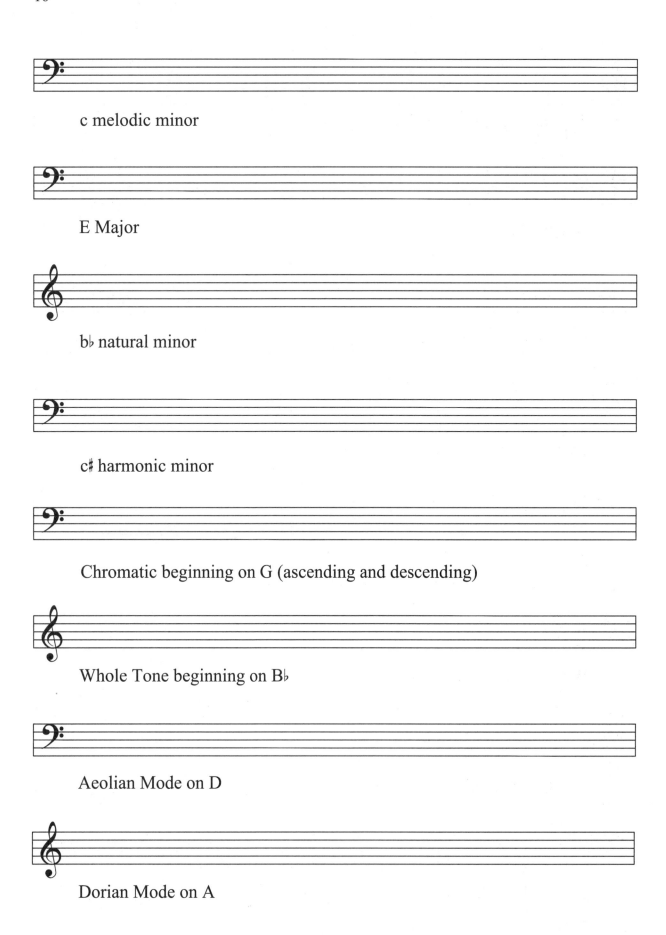

16

c melodic minor

E Major

b♭ natural minor

c♯ harmonic minor

Chromatic beginning on G (ascending and descending)

Whole Tone beginning on B♭

Aeolian Mode on D

Dorian Mode on A

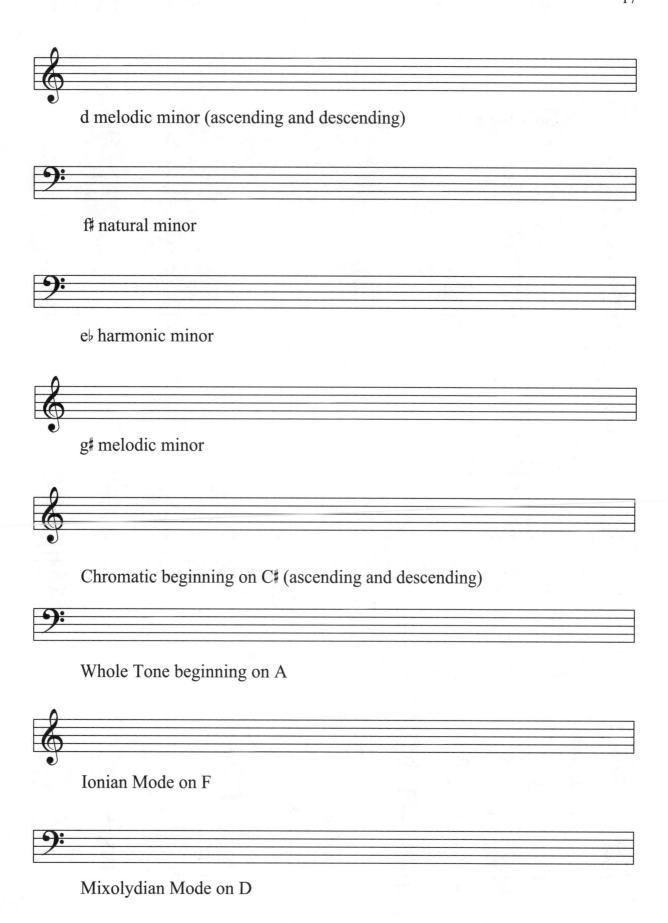

d melodic minor (ascending and descending)

f♯ natural minor

e♭ harmonic minor

g♯ melodic minor

Chromatic beginning on C♯ (ascending and descending)

Whole Tone beginning on A

Ionian Mode on F

Mixolydian Mode on D

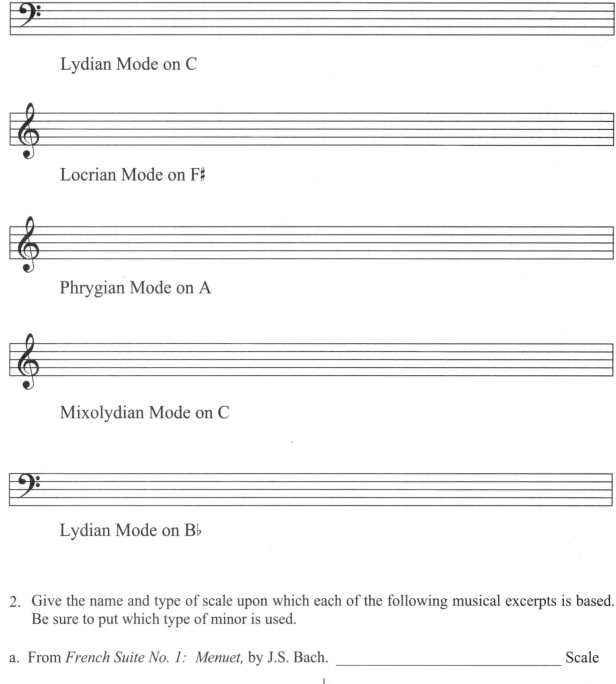

Lydian Mode on C

Locrian Mode on F♯

Phrygian Mode on A

Mixolydian Mode on C

Lydian Mode on B♭

2. Give the name and type of scale upon which each of the following musical excerpts is based. Be sure to put which type of minor is used.

a. From *French Suite No. 1: Menuet,* by J.S. Bach. _____ Scale

19

b. From *Sonata, K. 279,* by Mozart. _____ Scale

c. From *Sonata No. 32* by Scarlatti. _____ Scale

d. From *Sonata, XVI:34,* by Haydn. _____ Scale

e. From *Aufschwung* by Schumann. _____ Scale

20

f. From *Sonata, XVI:40* by Haydn. _____ Scale

g. From *Invention No. 4* by J.S. Bach. _____ Scale

h. From *Sonata, XVI:40,* by Haydn. _____ Scale

i. From *Sonata, XVI:42,* by Haydn. _____ Scale

LESSON 3
INTERVALS

An **INTERVAL** is the distance between two notes. In music, intervals are named with numbers. When naming intervals, count the two notes that make the interval, and all the lines and spaces, or all the letter names, between the two.

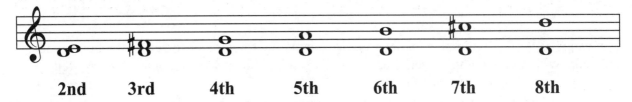

2nd   3rd   4th   5th   6th   7th   8th

If the top note of the interval is within the key of the bottom note, the interval is **Major** or **Perfect**. 2nds, 3rds, 6ths, and 7ths are Major. 4ths, 5ths, and 8ths are perfect.

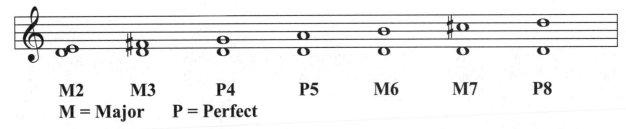

M2   M3   P4   P5   M6   M7   P8
M = Major   P = Perfect

If a Major 2nd, 3rd, 6th, or 7th is made smaller by lowering the top note or raising the bottom note a half step, without changing the letter name of either note, the interval becomes **minor**.

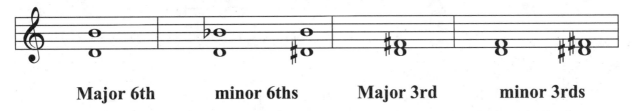

Major 6th   minor 6ths   Major 3rd   minor 3rds

If a Perfect 4th, 5th, or 8th is made smaller by lowering the top note or raising the bottom note a half step, without changing the letter name of either note, the interval becomes **diminished**.

Perfect 5th   diminished 5ths   Perfect 4th   diminished 4ths

If a Major 2nd, 3rd, 6th, or 7th is made smaller by lowering the top note or raising the bottom note a whole step, without changing the letter name of either note, the interval becomes **diminished**.

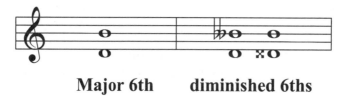

Major 6th   diminished 6ths

If a Major or Perfect interval is made larger by raising the top note or lowering the bottom note a half step, without changing the letter name of either note, the interval becomes **Augmented.**

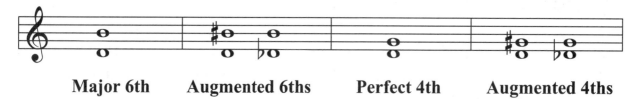

Major 6th   Augmented 6ths   Perfect 4th   Augmented 4ths

To write an interval above a given note, determine the key signature for the lower note, and add any necessary accidentals. For Major or Perfect intervals, keep those accidentals. For minor, diminished, or Augmented intervals, raise or lower the top note without changing the letter name.

In the example below, an Augmented 4th above F is needed. F Major has B♭. The 4th is made Augmented by removing the B♭ (raising the note a half step).

A4 up   Answer: B

To write an interval below a given note, determine all possibilities the note could be. Then, determine which of those notes is the correct one for the quality of the interval needed.

In the example below, a minor 7th below C is needed. The three possibilities are D, D♭, and D♯. A minor 7th above D♭ is C♭, a minor 7th above D♯ is C♯, and a minor 7th above D is C. The answer is D.

m7 below C   Answer: D

1. Name these intervals. Give their qualities (Major, minor, Perfect, Augmented, or diminished), and number names (2nd, 3rd, etc.).

2. Complete these intervals. Do note change the given note.

A2 up   m6 down   d7 up   A5 down   A7 up   A8 up   M6 down   m6 down

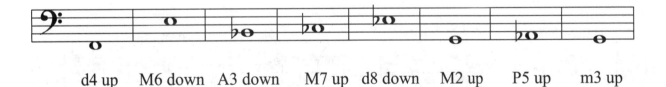

d4 up   M6 down   A3 down   M7 up   d8 down   M2 up   P5 up   m3 up

When naming intervals within music literature, follow these steps:

a. Write the sharps or flats from the key signature, or from earlier in the measure, before the notes (as reminders).

b. Determine the number for the interval (by counting the lines and spaces, or the letter names).

c. Using the key signature for the <u>lowest note of the interval</u>, find the quality (Major, minor, Perfect, diminished, or Augmented).

3. Name the circled intervals in the passages below. Follow the steps listed above for each interval.

a. From *Nocturne, Op. posth. 72, No. 1, by Chopin.*

b. From *Sonata, XVI:19,* by Haydn.

c. From *Sinfonia No. 3* by J.S. Bach.

LESSON 4
DIATONIC AND CHROMATIC HALF STEPS*

A piece of music is considered **DIATONIC** when it is based on a particular Major or minor key.

The term **DIATONIC HALF STEP** comes from the natural occurance of half steps in the Major scale. For example, in D Major Scale, diatonic half steps occur between F♯ and G, and between C♯ and D. In minor keys, half steps which include the harmonic or melodic minor notes are also diatonic. Some theory scholars use this as the definition for diatonic half step.

Another use of the term **DIATONIC HALF STEP** is to mean any half step which uses two different letter names, such as C♯ to D, or E to F. This is the definition used in this workbook. The diatonic half steps are circled in this example, from *Gathering of the Grapes--Happy Time!,* by Schumann.

CHROMATIC HALF STEPS are defined by some theory scholars as half steps which do not occur naturally within the scale.   For example, in a D Major scale, D to E♭ would be a chromatic half step, since it is not contained within the scale. The other definition is any half step that is written using the same letter name, such as C-C♯ or E♭ to E. This is the definition used in this workbook. The chromatic half steps are circled in the example below, from *Gathering of the Grapes--Happy Time!,* by Schumann.

*Scholarly theory texts are divided concerning the definition of diatonic and chromatic half steps.

IMPORTANT NOTE FOR CERTIFICATE OF MERIT™ STUDENTS: For your Certificate of Merit™ exam, use this definition: Diatonic half steps are half steps written using two different letter names, and chromatic half steps are half steps written using the same letter name, regardless of the context of the music.

1. Write half steps above these notes using two different letter names ("diatonic" half steps).

2. Write half steps above these notes using the same letter name ("chromatic" half steps).

3. Several half steps are circled in the examples below. Tell whether each is a diatonic or chromatic half step.

a. From *Sinfonia No. 9* by J.S. Bach.

_____   _____   _____   _____

b. From *Waltz, Op. 3, No. 3,* by Britten.

_____   _____   _____   _____   _____

c. From *French Suite No. 1: Menuet,* by J.S. Bach.

_____ _____   _____ _____

d. From *Sonata, XVI:40,* by Haydn.

LESSON 5
MAJOR, MINOR AUGMENTED AND DIMINISHED TRIADS AND INVERSIONS

A **TRIAD** is a chord which contains three notes.

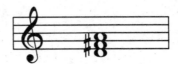

D Major Triad

MAJOR TRIADS are made up of the first, third, and fifth notes of the Major scale with the same letter name. The lowest note of a Major triad in root position (see example) names the triad.

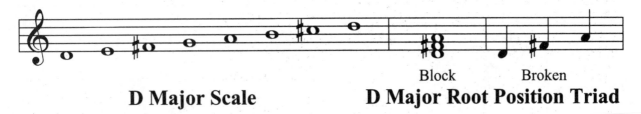

Block   Broken

D Major Scale   **D Major Root Position Triad**

To change a Major triad into a **MINOR** triad, lower the middle note (the third) a half step. Minor triads have the same sharps or flats found in the minor key signature with the same letter name.

D Major Triad   **d minor triad**

To change a Major triad into an **AUGMENTED** triad, raise the top note (the fifth) a half step. The intervals between the notes are both Major 3rds.

D Major Triad   **D Augmented Triad**

To change a Major triad into a **DIMINISHED** triad, lower the middle note (the third) <u>and</u> the top note (the fifth) a half step each. The intervals between the notes are both minor 3rds.

D Major Triad   **d diminished triad**

A **ROOT POSITION TRIAD** occurs when the note which names the triad is on the bottom. Root position triads are called $\frac{5}{3}$ triads, because when the triad is in its simplest position, the intervals from the bottom note are a 5th and a 3rd. When labelling a triad in root position, only the letter name and quality are needed.

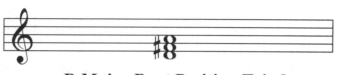

D Major Root Position Triad
(Labeled D Major or D Major $\frac{5}{3}$)

A **FIRST INVERSION TRIAD** occurs when the **third** or **middle** note of the triad is the lowest note. First inversion triads are called $\frac{6}{3}$ triads, because when they are in their simplest position (with the notes close together) they contain the intervals of a 6th and a 3rd above the bottom note.

When labelling first inversion triads, the symbol 6 (or $\frac{6}{3}$) is used beside the name of the triad.

D Major Root Position Triad   **D Major First Inversion Triad**
(Labeled D Major ^{6} or D Major $\frac{6}{3}$)

A **SECOND INVERSION TRIAD** occurs when the **fifth** or **top** note of the triad is on the bottom. Second inversion triads are called $\frac{6}{4}$ triads, because when they are in their simplest position (with the notes close together) they contain the intervals of a 6th and a 4th above the bottom note.

When labelling second inversion triads, the symbol $\frac{6}{4}$ is used beside the name of the triad.

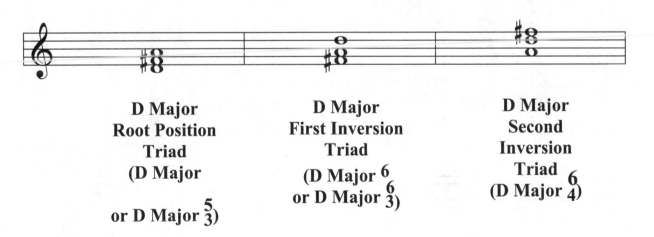

D Major   **D Major**   **D Major**
Root Position   **First Inversion**   **Second**
Triad   **Triad**   **Inversion**
(D Major   **(D Major ^{6}**   **Triad**
                           or D Major $\frac{6}{3}$)   **(D Major $\frac{6}{4}$)**
or D Major $\frac{5}{3}$)

32

1. Write these triads in root position, first inversion, and second inversion.

A♭ Major   c minor

G Major   e♭ diminished

E Augmented   b♭ diminished

A Augmented   d diminished

c♯ minor   F Major

F♯ Augmented   B Major

2. Name these triads with their letter names, qualities, and inversions.

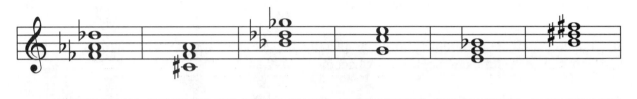

_____ _____ _____ _____ _____ _____

_____ _____ _____ _____ _____ _____

_____ _____ _____ _____ _____ _____

3. Write these triads.

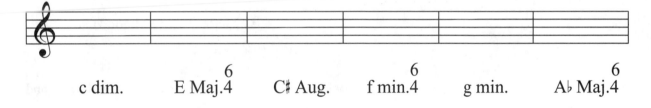

c dim.   E Maj.⁶₄   C♯ Aug.   f min.⁶₄   g min.   A♭ Maj.⁶₄

B Aug.⁶   d dim.⁶   f♯ dim.   B♭ Maj.⁶₄   E♭ Aug.⁶₄   a min.

F Maj.⁶   C Maj.⁶₄   c♯ min.⁶   e min.⁶   D Aug.   e♭ dim.⁶

In actual music, triads are rarely in their simplest positions. To determine the letter name and quality of a triad within a piece, follow these steps:

a. Put the triad in its simplest form by placing the letter names so that there is one letter between each (for example, F-C-F-A becomes F-A-C).

b. Add all sharps or flats from the key signature, or from earlier in the measure, to the letter names.

c. Determine the letter name and quality of the triad.

d. Determine the inversion of the triad by looking at the lowest note on the <u>lowest</u> staff.

Example (From *Minuet in G* by Beethoven):

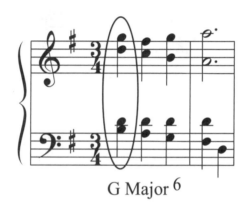

G Major ^{6}

a. Notes are B-D-D-G.

b. Simplest form is G-B-D.

c. G Major Triad.

d. B is the lowest note (in the bass clef), so the triad is in first inversion (6/3).

e. G Major ^{6} (or G Major $^6_3$)

4. Name the circled triads in the examples below by giving their letter names, qualitites, and inversions.

a. From *Sonata, Op. 14, No. 1,* by Beethoven.

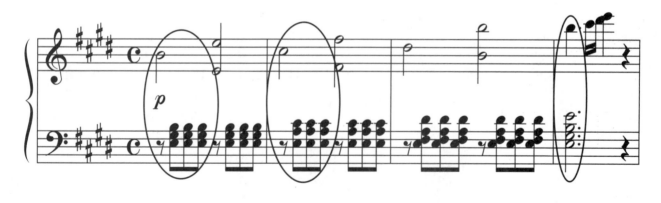

_____   _____   _____

b. From *Rhapsody, Op. 119, No. 4,* by Brahms.

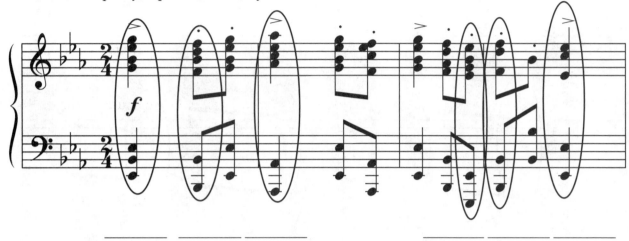

c. From *French Suite No. 1: Menuet,* by J.S. Bach.

d. From *Sonata No. 32* by Scarlatti.

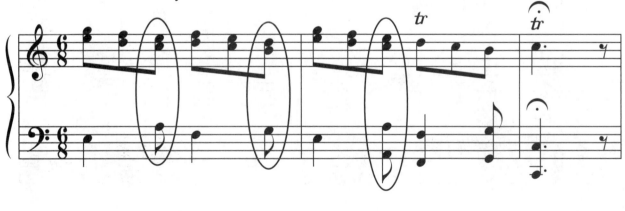

36

e. From *Aufschwung* by Schumann.

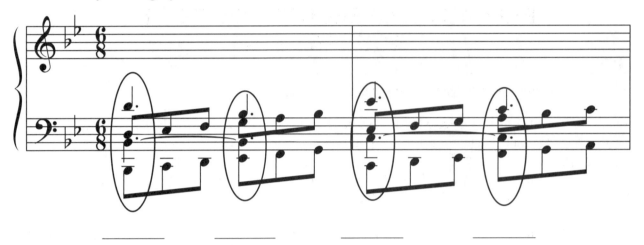

f. From *Sonata, K. 280,* by Mozart.

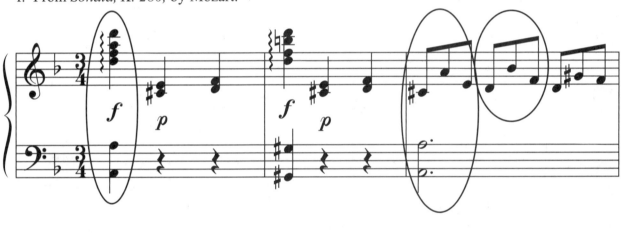

g. From *Sonata, K. 283,* by Mozart.

LESSON 6
PRIMARY AND SECONDARY TRIADS
FIGURED BASS

A triad can be built on each note of the scale.

When building triads on scale tones, all of the sharps or flats that are in the key being used must be added to the chords which have those notes.

Example: D Major Scale has F♯ and C♯. When writing the triads of D Major, every time an F or C appears in a chord, a sharp must be added to it. (See example below.)

Triads of the scale are numbered using Roman Numerals. Upper case Roman Numerals are used for Major triads, lower case Roman Numerals are used for minor triads, upper case Roman Numerals with "+" are used for Augmented triads, and lower case Roman Numerals with "o" are used for diminished triads. These are called the **FIGURED BASS SYMBOLS.**

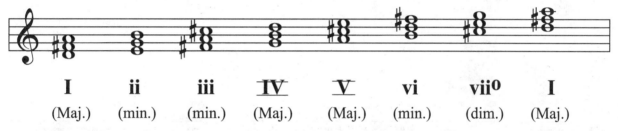

I	ii	iii	IV	V	vi	vii⁰	I
(Maj.)	(min.)	(min.)	(Maj.)	(Maj.)	(min.)	(dim.)	(Maj.)

PRIMARY AND SECONDARY TRIADS IN THE KEY OF D MAJOR

I, IV, and V are the **PRIMARY TRIADS**. In Major keys, these three triads are Major, and are the most commonly used chords for harmonizing tonal melodies. The chords are labelled with upper case Roman Numerals.

ii, iii, vi, and vii⁰ are the **SECONDARY TRIADS**. In Major keys, ii, iii, and vi are minor, and vii⁰ is diminished. The chords are labelled with lower case Roman Numerals, and the vii⁰ chord has a small circle beside the Roman Numeral.

The qualities of the triads in minor keys are different from those for Major keys. When using **harmonic minor**, the triads have the following qualities:

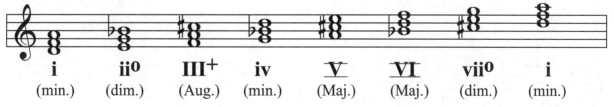

i	ii⁰	III⁺	iv	V	VI	vii⁰	i
(min.)	(dim.)	(Aug.)	(min.)	(Maj.)	(Maj.)	(dim.)	(min.)

PRIMARY AND SECONDARY TRIADS IN THE KEY OF D MINOR

The triads of the Whole Tone Scale all sound augmented, but the triads should be written using the scale tones, not as root position triads. (There are only seven chords, since there are only seven scale degrees.)

TRIADS OF THE WHOLE TONE SCALE ON D

1. Write the Primary and Secondary Triads for these keys, and label the triads with Roman Numerals. Circle each Primary Triad, and put a box around each Secondary Triad. Do not use a key signature. Write the sharps or flats before the notes. (The first one is given.)

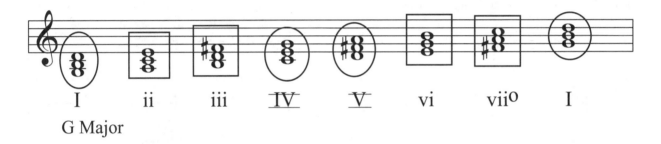

I   ii   iii   IV   V   vi   vii°   I

G Major

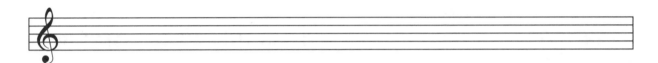

D♭ Major

Whole Tone on A (Do not circle chords or write Roman Numerals)

B♭ Major

g♯ minor

Whole Tone on F (Do not circle chords or write Roman Numerals)

b minor

G♭ Major

f♯ minor

C♭ Major

Whole Tone on C (Do not circle chords or write Roman Numerals)

40

2. Write the Primary Triads for these keys, and label the triads with Roman Numerals. Do not use a key signature. Write the sharps or flats before the notes. (The first one is given.)

C Major   D Major

Eb Major   e minor

f minor   F# Major

c# minor   Ab Major

eb minor   A Major

G Major   Bb Major

3. Write the Secondary Triads for these keys, and label the triads with Roman Numerals. Do not use a key signature. Write the sharps or flats before the notes. (The first one is given.)

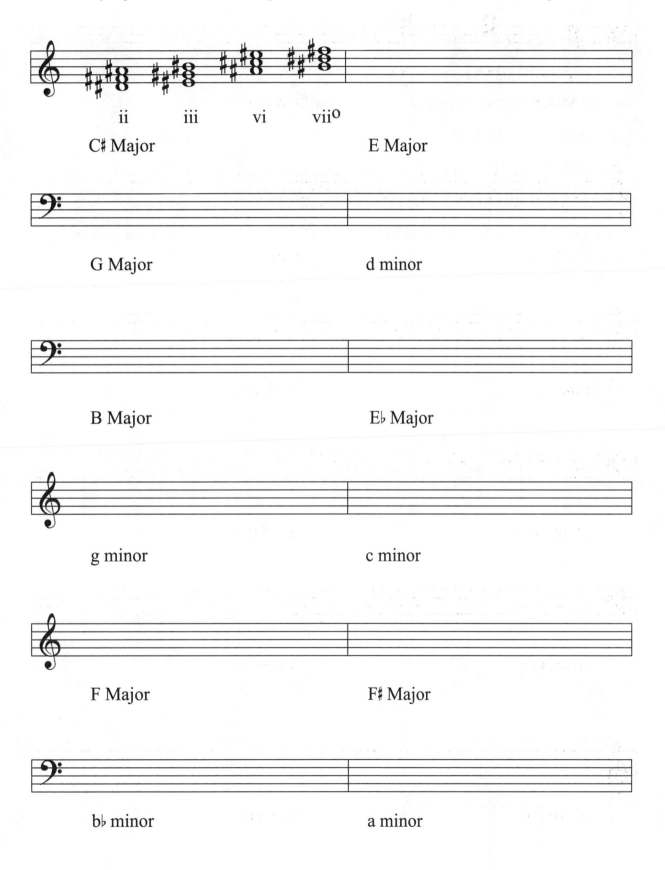

ii   iii   vi   viiᵒ

C♯ Major   E Major

G Major   d minor

B Major   E♭ Major

g minor   c minor

F Major   F♯ Major

b♭ minor   a minor

Each degree of the scale has a name. These are called the **SCALE DEGREE NAMES:**

The **I** chord is **TONIC.**

The **ii** chord is **SUPERTONIC.**

The **iii** chord is **MEDIANT.**

The **IV** chord is **SUBDOMINANT.**

The **V** chord is **DOMINANT.**

The **vi** chord is **SUBMEDIANT.**

The **vii^o** chord is **LEADING TONE.**

(Note: Qualities used above are from Major keys. The names stay the same when in minor.)

4. Match these Roman Numerals with their scale degree names.

a. ii   _____ Submediant

b. I   _____ Dominant

c. iii   _____ Supertonic

d. vii^o _____ Subdominant

e. IV   _____ Leading Tone

f. vi   _____ Mediant

g. V   _____ Tonic

5. Write the scale degree names for these Roman Numerals.

I   _____

ii   _____

iii   _____

IV   _____

V   _____

vi   _____

vii^o _____

In actual music, chords are rarely in their simplest position. To determine the Roman Numeral of a chord within a piece, do the following:

a.   Determine the Major or minor key of the piece.

b.   Put the chord in its simplest form by placing the letter names so that there is one letter between each (for example, F-C-F-A becomes F-A-C).

c.   Add all sharps or flats from the key signature or from earlier in the measure to the letter names.

d.   Determine the Roman Numeral of the chord by counting from the letter name of the key up to the name of the chord.

e.   Determine the inversion of the chord by looking at the lowest note (on the <u>lowest</u> staff).

Example (From *Minuet in G* by Beethoven):

V6

a.   Key of G Major

b.   Notes are: F♯-D-A-A

c.   Simplest form is: D-F♯-A

d.   D Major Triad. The piece is in the key of G Major. D is the fifth note of the G Major Scale; therefore, this is the V chord.

e.   The lowest note (in the bass clef) is F♯. The chord is in first inversion. Label the chord V^6_3, or V^6 as an abbreviation.

44

6. Label the circled chords below. Put the Figured Bass symbol (the Roman Numeral and inversion) for each.

a. From *Sonata, K. 284,* by Mozart. Key of: _____

_____   _____   _____

_____   _____   _____

b. From *Sonata No. 40* by Scarlatti. Key of: _____

_____   _____   _____   _____

c. From *Grillen* by Schumann. Key of: _____

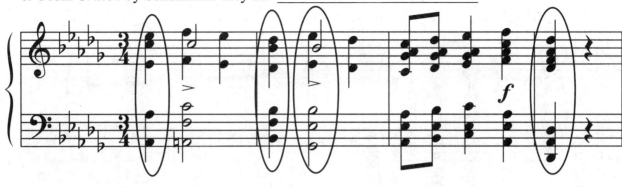

_____   _____   _____   _____

d. From *French Suite No. 3: Menuet II,* by J.S. Bach. Key of: _____

_____   _____

e. From *Sonata, K. 281,* by Mozart. Key of: _____

_____   _____

46

f. From *Sonata, Hob. XVI:42,* by Haydn. Key of: _____

LESSON 7
SEVENTH CHORDS

SEVENTH CHORDS are chords which contain four different notes, and are made up of a triad plus the interval of 7th above the root.

The **DOMINANT SEVENTH CHORD** is created when a fourth note is added to the V chord (the Dominant chord). This fourth note is a seventh above the root of the chord, giving it the name "Dominant 7th." The chord consists of a Major triad on the bottom, with the added interval of a minor 7th.

DOMINANT 7TH   D MAJOR   MINOR 7TH   DOMINANT 7TH
                    TRIAD   CHORD ON D

The Dominant Seventh is so named because it is based on the V or Dominant chord, and has the interval of a 7th within the chord.

Inversions of the Dominant Seventh chord are:

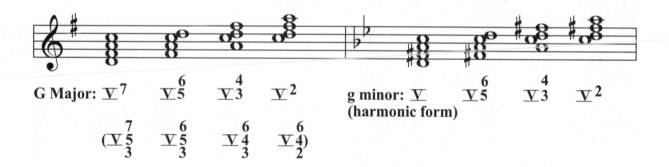

Dominant Seventh chords can be on a given note, or in a given key. When asked to write a Dominant Seventh on a given note, write a Major triad on that note, and add a minor seventh.

To write a Dominant Seventh within a given key, find the fifth note of the key (the dominant), and write a V chord. Add the note which is a minor 7th above the <u>root</u> of the chord. When in harmonic minor, the third of the chord (which is the leading tone or 7th of the key) must be raised a half step.

DOMINANT 7TH ON D   **DOMINANT 7TH IN THE KEY OF D MAJOR**

48

1. Write Dominant Seventh chords and their inversions in the following keys, and label the chords with Roman Numerals.

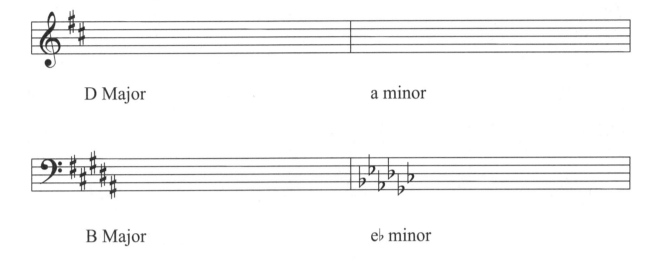

D Major   a minor

B Major   e♭ minor

2. Write Dominant Seventh chords and their inversions on these notes.

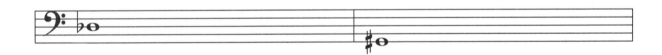

MAJOR SEVENTH CHORDS consist of a Major triad and a Major 7th above the root. When writing Major Seventh chords, add all sharps or flats which are contained in the Major key signature of the root.

D Major Triad   Major 7th   D Major
Seventh Chord

MAJOR SEVENTH CHORD ON D

3. Write these Major Seventh chords and their inversions.

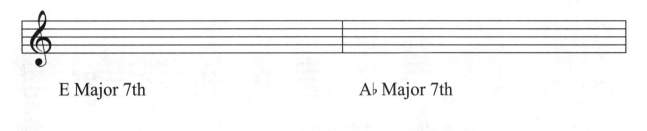

E Major 7th   A♭ Major 7th

F♯ Major 7th   B Major 7th

MINOR SEVENTH CHORDS contain a minor triad and the interval of a minor seventh above the root. When writing minor seventh chords, add the sharps or flats from the natural minor key signature of the root.

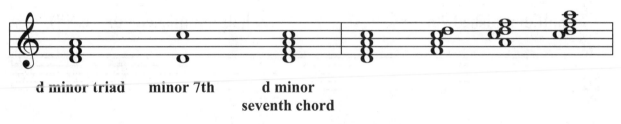

d minor triad   minor 7th   d minor
                              seventh chord

MINOR SEVENTH CHORD ON D

4. Write these minor seventh chords and their inversions.

a minor 7th   e♭ minor 7th

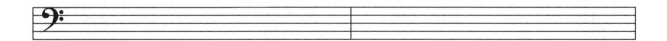

b minor 7th   c minor 7th

50

HALF DIMINISHED SEVENTH CHORDS consist of a diminished triad, and a minor seventh above the root.

d diminished   minor 7th   d diminished
triad   seventh chord

HALF DIMINISHED SEVENTH CHORD ON D
(d⌀7)

5. Write these half diminished seventh chords and their inversions.

g half diminished 7th (g⌀7)   e♭ half diminished 7th (e♭⌀7)

a half diminished 7th (a⌀7)   c half diminished 7th (c⌀7)

The **DIMINISHED SEVENTH CHORD** consists of a diminished triad, with the interval of a diminished seventh added to the top.

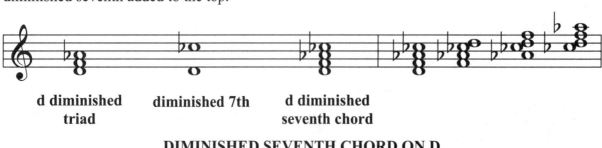
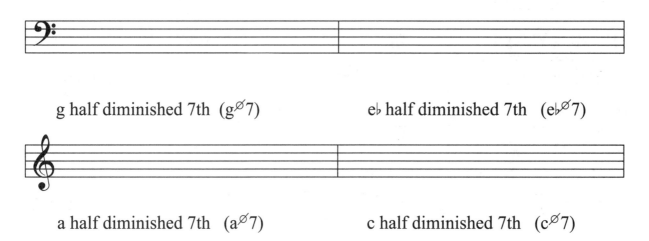

d diminished   diminished 7th   d diminished
triad   seventh chord

DIMINISHED SEVENTH CHORD ON D
(d°7)

6. Write these diminished 7th chords and their inversions.

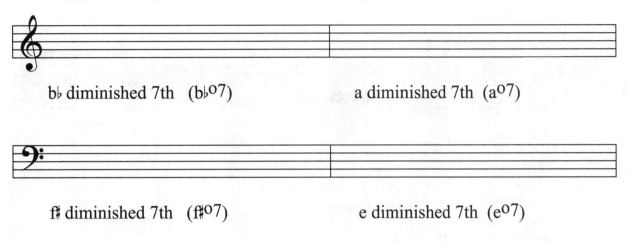

bb diminished 7th (bb^o7)   a diminished 7th (a^o7)

f# diminished 7th (f#^o7)   e diminished 7th (e^o7)

7. Label these seventh chords with their letter names, qualities, and inversions.

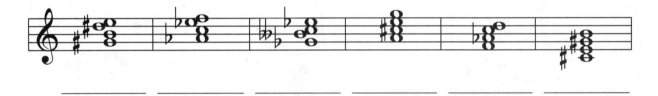

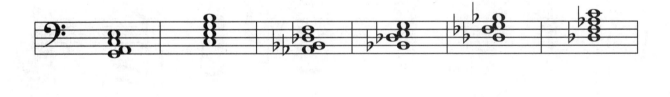

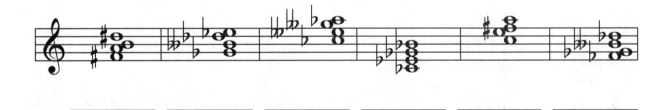

52

8. Label the circled seventh chords in the examples below with their letter names, qualities, and inversions (figured bass). (The first one is given.)

a. From *Invention No. 14* by J.S. Bach.

$$\text{B}\flat \text{ Dominant } {}^4_3$$

b. From *Nocturne, Op. posth. 72, No. 1,* by Chopin.

_____

c. From *Rhapsody, Op. 119, No. 4,* by Brahms.

_____   _____

d. From *Sonata, Hob. XVI:34,* by Haydn.

_____

e. From *Invention No. 4* by J.S. Bach.

f. From *Sonata, K. 280,* by Mozart.

g. From *Sonata No. 40* by Scarlatti.

h. From *Three Rondos* by Bartok.

54

i. From *Grillen* by Schumann.

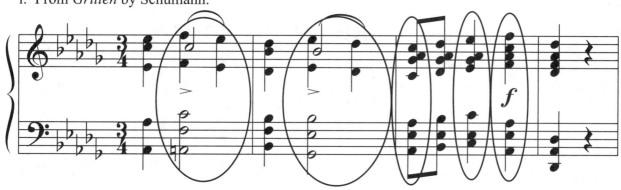

j. From *Three Rondos* by Bartok.

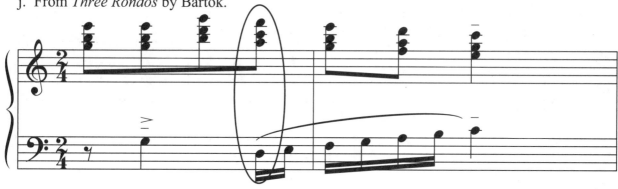

k. From *French Suite No. 3: Menuet II,* by J.S. Bach.

l. From *Three Rondos* by Bartok.

LESSON 8
THE SECONDARY DOMINANT

Many times, a composer will use chords which are not within the key of the piece of music. One of the most common of these is the **SECONDARY DOMINANT**.

The Secondary Dominant is so named because it is the Dominant (V) of a key other than Tonic (I). It is usually followed by the chord which would be a I chord of the key to which it belongs. The qualities of secondary dominants are different from those of the regular primary and secondary triads.

Examples in the key of C Major (note that two different ways of labelling the chords are shown; the most typical type of labelling is the second type shown here):

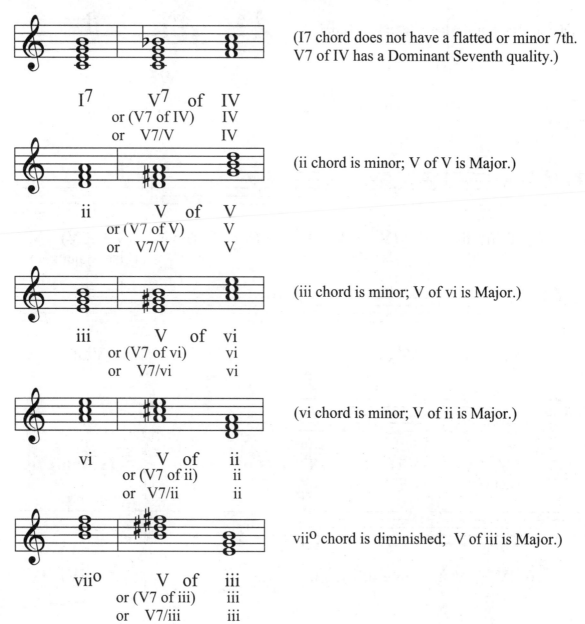

(I7 chord does not have a flatted or minor 7th.
V7 of IV has a Dominant Seventh quality.)

I^7 V^7 of IV
or (V7 of IV) IV
or V7/V IV

(ii chord is minor; V of V is Major.)

ii V of V
or (V7 of V) V
or V7/V V

(iii chord is minor; V of vi is Major.)

iii V of vi
or (V7 of vi) vi
or V7/vi vi

(vi chord is minor; V of ii is Major.)

vi V of ii
or (V7 of ii) ii
or V7/ii ii

vii° chord is diminished; V of iii is Major.)

vii° V of iii
or (V7 of iii) iii
or V7/iii iii

56

1. Write these Secondary Dominants. Determine whether to use the Major or minor key by the quality of the second Roman Numeral. V of V examples have "Major" or "minor" written below them. Remember to use harmonic minor. Follow the steps in the example below to write each one.

a. Find the chord which represents the <u>second</u> Roman Numeral (for example, for V of IV, find the IV chord of the given key).

b. Find the V (or V7) chord for that second chord. (For example, if the IV chord is C Major, count up five notes to G Major chord.

c. Write the Secondary Dominant chord, followed by the chord represented by the second Roman Numeral.

Example: V^6_5 of iii in the key of A Major.

a. Find the iii chord in A Major: c♯ minor chord.

b. Find the V7 chord of c♯ minor: G♯7.

c. Write G♯ $^6_5$ (the inversion of G♯7) followed by c♯ minor (the iii chord).

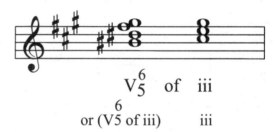

V^6_5 of iii

or (V5 of iii)   iii

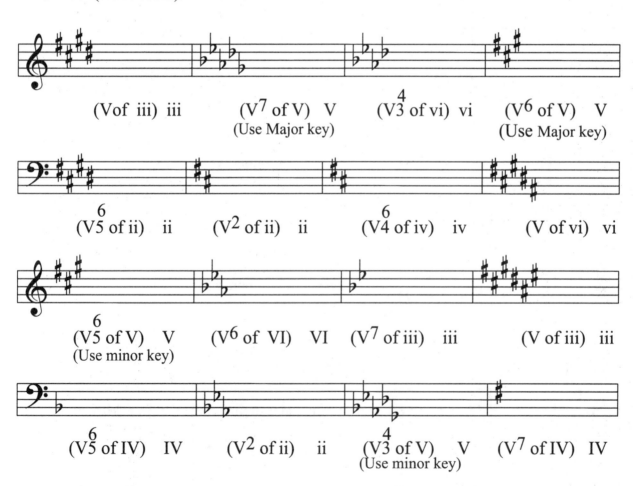

When labelling Secondary Dominants in music literature, follow these steps:

a. Determine the Major or minor key of the piece.

b. Label the Secondary Dominant (the first of the two chords) with the Roman Numeral V, and the inversion number (for example, V, V7, V 6/5, etc.), followed by "of _____," using the Roman Numeral for the second chord to fill the blank.

c. Label the second chord with its Roman Numeral and figured bass symbol (the inversion numbers, such as 6, 6/4, etc.).

d. The two chords will be labelled, for example, "(V of iii)   iii."

Example: From *A Little Canon* by Schumann.

a. Key of A Major.

b. The first chord's letter name is A Dominant 7th. Label the chord V7.

c. The second chord's letter name is D Major. This is the IV chord in A Major. The chord is in second inversion. Label the chord IV $\frac{6}{4}$.

d. Chords are labelled "(V7 of IV)   IV $\frac{6}{4}$," or V7/IV   IV$\frac{6}{4}$.

$$(\text{V}^7 \text{ of IV}) \text{ IV}\!\overset{6}{4}$$

$$\text{or V7 of IV }\overset{6}{4}$$

$$\text{or V7/IV   IV}\!\overset{6}{4}$$

58

2. Label the Secondary Dominants in these excerpts with "V of," then label the following chord with its Roman Numeral. (Be sure to add the figured bass symbols, that is, the inversion numbers, to all chords.)

a. From *French Suite No. 1: Menuet,* by J.S. Bach. Key of: _____ minor

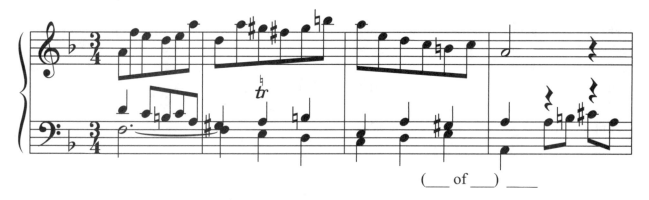

(___ of ___) ___

b. From *Sonata, Hob. XVI:40,* by Haydn. Key of: _____ Major

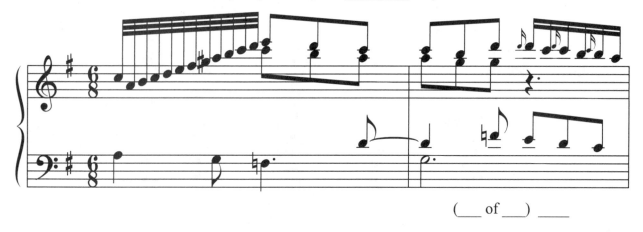

(___ of ___) ____

c. From *Sonata, K. 283,* by Mozart. Key of: _____ Major

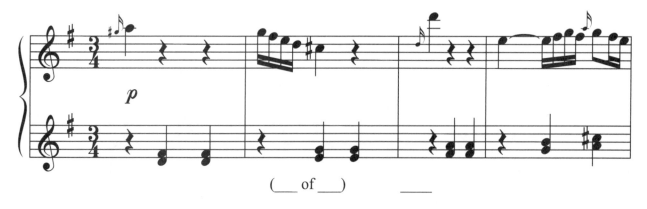

(___ of ___)   ____

d. From *Grillen* by Schumann. Key of: _____ Major

(__ of __)   ____

e. From *French Suite No. 3, Menuet II,* by J.S. Bach. Key of: _____ minor

(__ of __) ___ (__ of __)   ___   (__ of __) ____

f. From *Sonata, K. 280,* by Mozart. Key of: _____ Major

(__ of __)   ___

g. From *Sonata, Hob. XVI:42,* by Haydn. Key of: _____ Major

(___ of ___) ____

h. From *Sonata, Op. 2, No. 1,* by Beethoven. Key of _____ Major

(___ of ___) ____

i. From *Sonata, Op. 2, No. 1,* by Beethoven. Key of: _____ Major

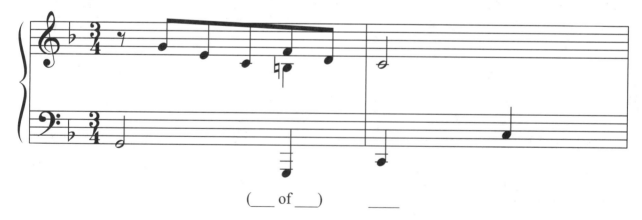

(___ of ___)   ____

LESSON 9
AUTHENTIC, HALF, PLAGAL, AND DECEPTIVE CADENCES; CHORD PROGRESSIONS

A **CADENCE** is a closing or ending for a musical phrase, made up of a combination of chords. There are many types of cadences. Four common cadences are:

AUTHENTIC, HALF, PLAGAL, and DECEPTIVE CADENCES

An **AUTHENTIC CADENCE** consists of a V or V^7 chord followed by a I chord:

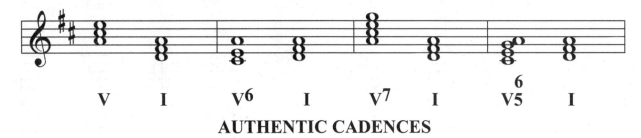

AUTHENTIC CADENCES

A **PLAGAL CADENCE** consists of a IV chord followed by a I chord:

PLAGAL CADENCES

A **HALF CADENCE** is a cadence which ends with a V or V^7 chord:

HALF CADENCES

A **DECEPTIVE CADENCE** consists of a V (or sometimes IV) chord followed by a vi chord:

DECEPTIVE CADENCES

1. Write the following cadences. Determine whether to use the Major or minor key by
   thequality of the Roman Numerals.

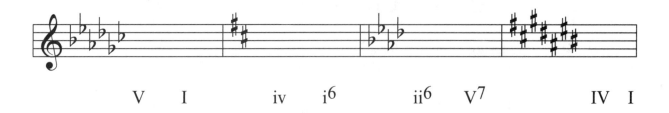

V   I   iv   i⁶   ii⁶   V⁷   IV   I

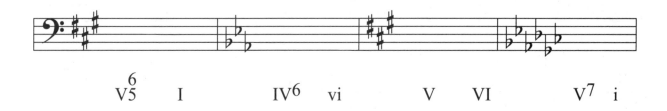

iv   VI   V   vi   V$^6_4$ i⁶   i$^6_4$ V

V$^6_5$ I   IV⁶   vi   V   VI   V⁷   i

iv$^6_4$ i   V of V V   IV⁶   I$^6_4$ i   V

63

2. Label the chords of each of these cadences with Roman Numerals and figured bass, then put the type of cadence (Authentic, Half, Plagal, or Deceptive) on the line below the Roman Numerals.

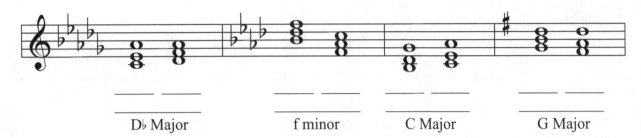

Db Major   f minor   C Major   G Major

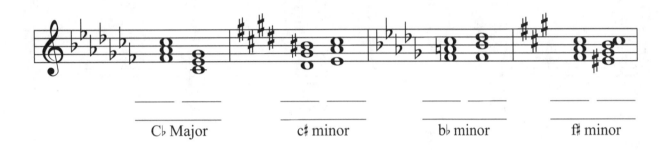

Cb Major   c# minor   bb minor   f# minor

b minor   F# Major   c minor   F Major

g minor   D Major   Eb Major   a minor

A **CHORD PROGRESSION** or **MIXED CADENCE** is created by combining certain chords from a given key. A smooth progression is created by using **common tones** (notes that remain the same when the chord changes). The following chord progression **MODULATES** to a new key. A secondary dominant is used to transition into the new key. (See more on modulation in Lesson 10.)

The **PIVOT CHORD** is a chord that precedes a chord change, and is common to both the original key and the key to which the music modulates. The pivot chord is circled in this example.

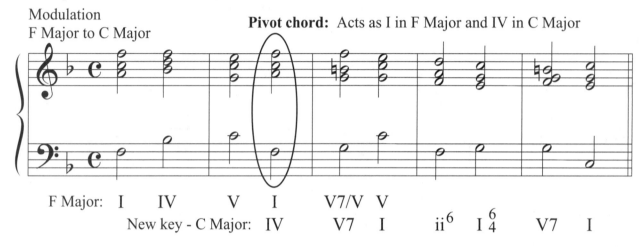

Modulation
F Major to C Major

Pivot chord: Acts as I in F Major and IV in C Major

F Major: I   IV   V   I   V7/V V

New key - C Major: IV   V7   I   ii^6 I$^6_4$ V7   I

3. a. Label the chords used in these chord progressions with Roman Numerals and figured bass.
   Circle the pivot chord in each example.

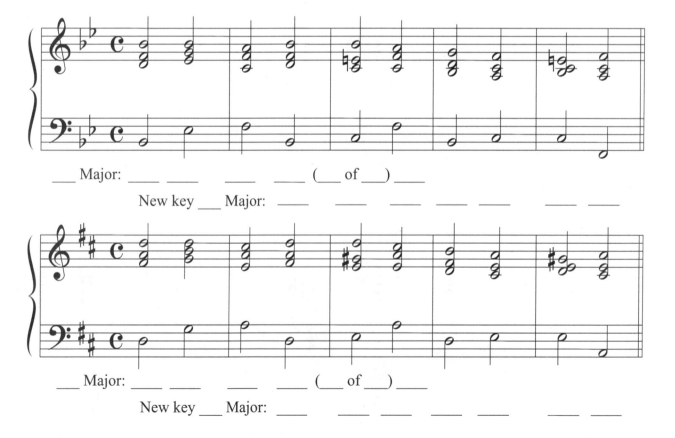

___ Major: ____ ____   ____   ____ (__ of __) ___

New key ___ Major: ____   ____   ____   ____   ____   ____

___ Major: ____ ____   ____   ____ (__ of __) ___

New key ___ Major: ____   ____   ____   ____   ____

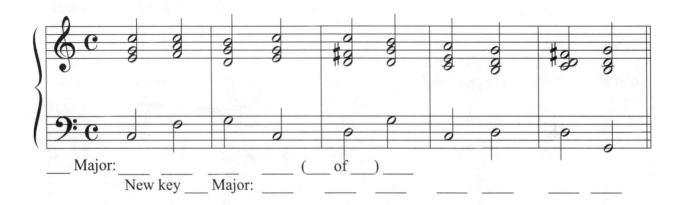

____ Major: ____ ____ ____ ____ (___ of ___) ___

New key ___ Major: ____ ____ ____ ____ ____ ____ ____

b. Write these chord progressions. Circle the pivot chord in each example.

___ Major: I   IV   V   I   V7/V   V

New key ___ Major: IV   V7   I   ii^6 I$^6_4$ V7   I

___ Major: I   IV   V   I   V7/V   V

New key ___ Major: IV   V7   I   ii^6 I$^6_4$ V7   I

___ Major: I   IV   V   I   V7/V   V

New key ___ Major: IV   V7   I   ii^6 I$^6_4$ V7   I

66

When labelling cadences in music literature, label the last two chords of a phrase with their Roman Numerals. These are the two chords which make up the cadence. Then, give the cadence its name (Authentic, Half, Plagal, or Deceptive).

Example (From *Waltz, Op. posth. 69, No. 1,* by Chopin.): Key of A♭ Major, Authentic Cadence

4. Name the cadence at the end of each phrase below. Give the name of the Major or minor key, write the Roman Numerals for the last two chords, and name the type of cadence (Authentic, Half, Plagal, or Deceptive).

a. From *Rhapsody, Op. 119, No. 4,* by Brahms.

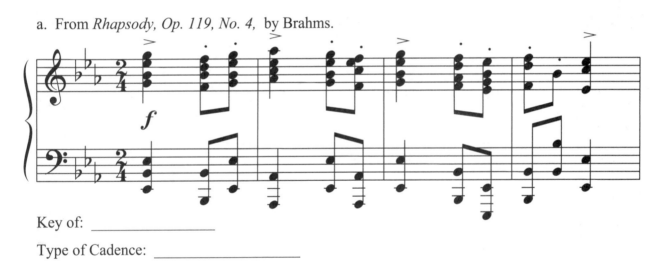

Key of: _____

Type of Cadence: _____

b. From *Sonata, Op. 10, No. 1,* by Beethoven.

Key of: _____

Type of Cadence: _____

c. From *Sonata, Op. 2, No. 1,* by Beethoven.

Key of: _____

Type of Cadence: _____

d. From *Sonata, K. 281,* by Mozart.

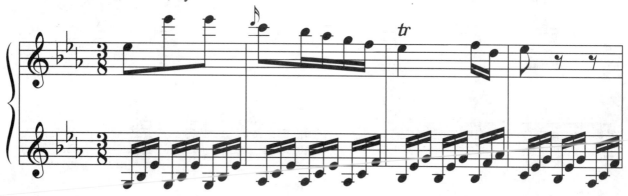

Key of: _____

Type of Cadence: _____

e. From *Sonata, K. 283,* by Mozart.

Key of: _____

Type of Cadence: _____

68

f. From *Sonata, Hob. XVI:42* by Haydn.

Key of: _____

Type of Cadence: _____

g. From *Sonata No. 32* by Scarlatti.

Key of: _____

Type of Cadence: _____

h. From *Sonata, . 284,* by Mozart.

Key of: _____

Type of Cadence: _____

LESSON 10
MODULATION

MODULATION occurs when a musical composition changes from the original key to another key, and remains in the new key for a reasonable amount of time.

A piece of music may modulate to any key, but frequently either the Dominant (V) key or the relative Major or minor is used.

In the example below, from *Song of War* by Schumann, the music begins in the key of D Major, and modulates to the key of F♯ Major.

Two important 20th Century theorists, Schoenberg and Schenker, taught that music does not truly modulate, but that sections of music which appear to modulate are essentially extended cadences, and that these sections are not much different in essence from sections which use any chord other than tonic.

1. In the following excerpts, give the name of the original key, and the name of the key to which the music modulates.

a. From *Sonata, Hob. XVI:41,* by Haydn.

Original key: _____ Modulates to: _____

b. From *Sonata, K. 279,* by Mozart.

Original key: _____ Modulates to: _____

(continued on p. 72)

c. From *Intermezzo, Op. 118, No. 2,* by Brahms.

Original key: _____ Modulates to: _____

74

d. From *Sonata (1766)* by Haydn.

Original key: _____ Modulates to: _____

REVIEW
TERMS USED IN LESSONS 1-10

Authentic Cadence: A V-I cadence (in harmomic minor, V-i).

Cadence: A closing or ending for a phrase of music, made up of two or more chords.

Chromatic Half Step: A half step which does not occur naturally within the key of the music.

Chromatic Scale: A scale made up entirely of half steps.

Deceptive Cadence: a V-vi cadence (in harmonic minor, V-VI).

Diatonic Half Step: A half step which occurs naturally within the key of the music.

Diminished Seventh Chord: A four note chord made up of a diminished triad, and a diminished 7th above the root.

Dominant Seventh: A four note chord made up of a Major triad, and a minor 7th above the root. Root position is V^7, first inversion is V 6/5, second inversion is V 4/3, and third inversion is V^2.

Figured Bass: Symbols used to denote the inversion of a chord (such as 6, 6/4, 6/5, 4/3, or 2).

First Inversion: A triad written with the third as the lowest note. The figured bass symbol for a triad in first inversion is 6/3, or 6. The figured bass symbol for a seventh chord in first in 6/5/3, or 6/5.

Half Cadence: A cadence which ends with the V chord.

Half Diminished Seventh Chord: A four note chord made up of a diminished triad, and the interval of a minor seventh.

Interval: The distance between two notes, named with numbers. Intervals may be Major, Perfect, minor, diminished, or Augmented.

Inversion: A triad written in a position in which the note that names the triad is not the lowest.

Key Signature: The sharps or flats at the beginning of a piece of music. (There are Major and minor key signatures.)

Major Seventh Chord: A four note chord made up of a Major triad and the interval of a Major seventh.

Minor Seventh Chord: A four note chord made up of a minor triad and the interval of a minor seventh.

Modes: Tonalities including Ionian, Dorian, Phrygian, Lydian, Mixolydian, Aeolian, and Locrian.

Modulation: A key change within a composition.

Pivot Chord: Used before a modulation, a chord that is common to both the original and the key to which the music modulates.

Plagal Cadence: A IV-I cadence (in harmonic minor, iv-i).

Primary Triads: The I, IV, and V chords. (In minor, i, iv, and V.)

Root Position: A traid written in a position so that the note which names it is the lowest. The figured bass symbol for a triad in root position is 5/3. The figured bass symbol for a seventh chord in root position is 7/5/3, or 7.

Scale: A series of notes in alphabetical order (for example, C-D-E-F-G-A-B-C).

Scale Degree Names: Tonic (I), Supertonic (ii), Mediant (iii), Subdominant (IV), Dominant (V), Submediant (vi), Leading Tone (vii^{o}).

Second Inversion: A triad written with the fifth as the lowest note. The figured bass symbol for a triad in second inversion is 6/4. The figured bass symbol for a seventh chord in second inversion is 6/4/3, or 4/3.

Secondary Dominant: The V or Dominant of a key other than Tonic (I).

Secondary Triads: The ii, iii, vi, and vii^{o} chords. (In harmonic minor, ii^{o}, III^{+}, VI, and vii^{o}).

Third Inversion: A seventh chord written with the seventh as the lowest note. The figured bass symbol for third inversion is 6/4/2, or 2.

Triad: A chord which contains three different notes, with qualities of Major, minor, Augmented, or diminished.

Whole Tone Scale: A scale made up entirely of whole steps.

Ionian mode: scale in which half steps occur between notes 3-4 and 7-8, like the major scale.

Dorian mode: scale in which half steps occur between notes 2-3 and 6-7, as if playing all white keys from D to D.

Phrygian mode: scale in which half steps occur between notes 1-2 and 5-6, as if playing all white keys from E to E.

Lydian mode: scale in which half steps occur between notes 4-5 and 7-8, as if playing all white keys from F to F.

Mixolydian mode: scale in which half steps occur between notes 3-4 and 6-7, as if playing all white keys from G to G.

Aeolian mode: scale in which half steps occur between notes 2-3 and 5-6, as if playing all white keys from A to A.

Locrian mode: scale in which half steps occur between notes 1-2 and 4-5, as if playing all white keys from B to B.

REVIEW
LESSONS 1-10

1. Name these Major keys.

_____ _____ _____ _____ _____ _____

2. Name these <u>minor</u> keys.

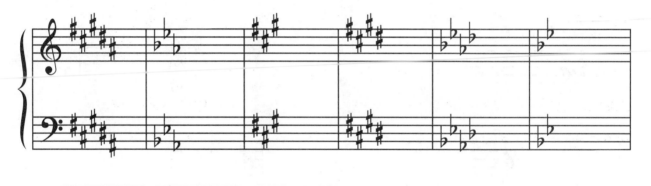

_____ _____ _____ _____ _____ _____

3. Write the key signatures for these keys, in both clefs.

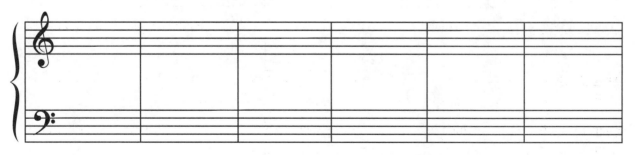

C♭ Major   C♯ Major   b♭ minor   d minor   E Major   b minor

4. Complete the Circle of Fifths.

5. Write these scales.

e melodic minor (ascending and descending)

Chromatic beginning on D (ascending and descending)

g natural minor

c♯ harmonic minor

Whole tone beginning on G

A♭ Major

Aeolian mode on E

Locrian mode on F♯

80

6. Name these intervals.

_____   _____   _____   _____   _____   _____   _____   _____

7. Complete these intervals.

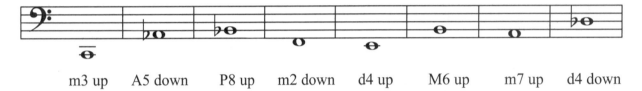

m3 up   A5 down   P8 up   m2 down   d4 up   M6 up   m7 up   d4 down

8. Write half steps above these notes, using two different letter names (Diatonic half steps).

9. Write half steps above these notes, using the same letter name (Chromatic half steps).

10. Label these triads with their letter names, qualities (Major, minor, Augmented, or diminished), and figured bass symbols (inversions).

_____   _____   _____   _____   _____   _____

11. Write these triads.

D♭ Maj.⁶   f♯ dim.⁶₄   B Maj.⁶₄   e♭ min   A♭ Aug.⁶   c min.

12. Write the primary triads for these keys, and label the triads with Roman Numerals.

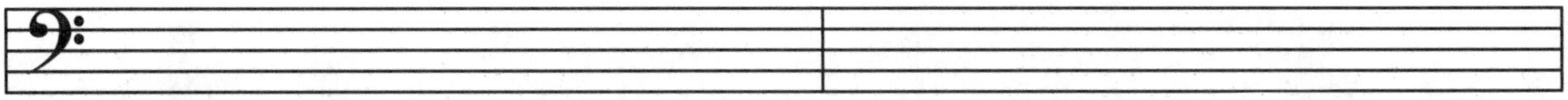

a minor

G Major

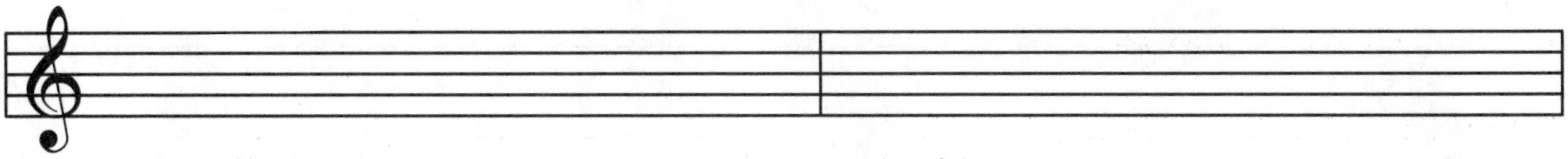

A♭ Major

c♯ minor

13. Write the secondary triads for these keys, and label the triads with Roman Numerals.

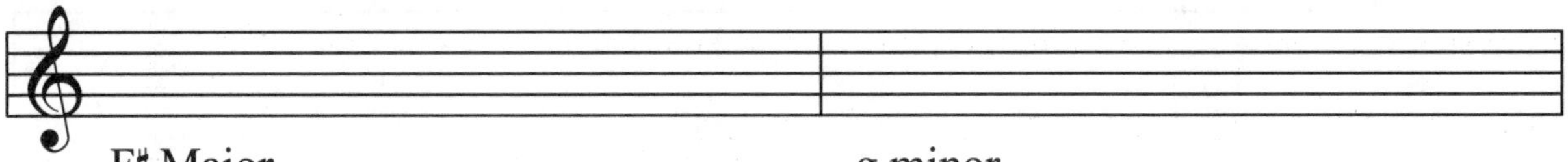

F♯ Major

g minor

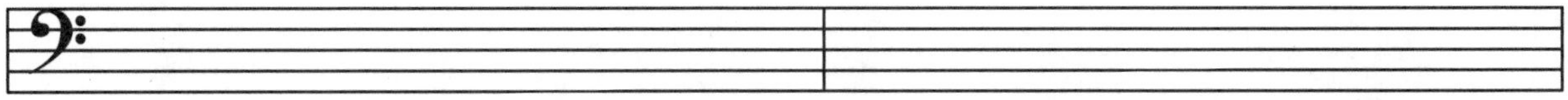

b minor

D Major

14. Write the triads of the whole tone scale, beginning on the given notes.

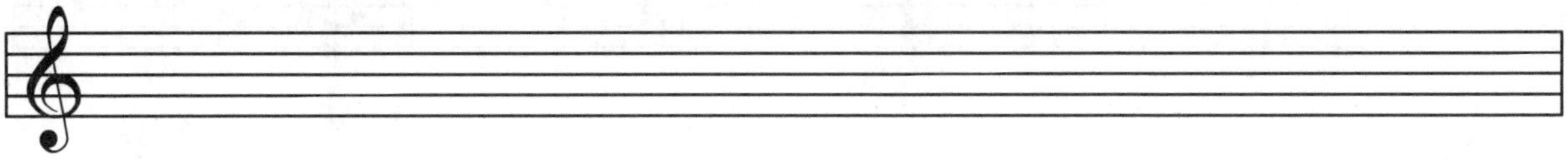

Beginning on C♯

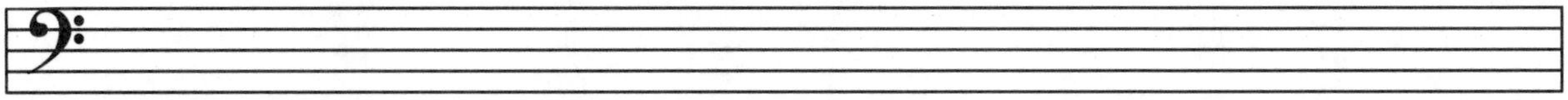

Beginning on A♭

15. Write the scale degree name for the following Roman Numerals.

a. I or i _____

b. ii or ii° _____

c. iii or III⁺ _____

d. IV or iv _____

e. V _____

f. V⁷ _____

g. vi or VI _____

h. vii° _____

16. Name the following seventh chords with their letter names and qualities (Major 7th, minor 7th, half diminished 7th, diminished 7th, or Dominant 7th). Be sure to include figured bass (inversion numbers).

_____ _____ _____ _____ _____ _____

17. Write these seventh chords.

c# min.³⁴   f min.⁵⁶   A Maj.²   E♭ Dom.²   b min.⁷   F# Dom.³⁴

18. Write the Roman Numerals (Figured Bass) for the following Secondary Dominants. (Determine each using the Major key signature.)

_____ of _____   _____ of _____   _____ of _____   _____ of _____

19 Write these Secondary Dominants.

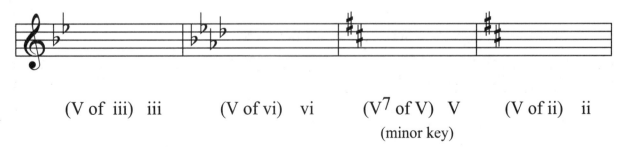

(V of iii) iii   (V of vi) vi   (V⁷ of V) V   (V of ii) ii

(minor key)

20. Label the chords used in the following cadences with their figured bass symbols, then write the name of the type of cadence.

_____ _____   _____ _____   _____ _____   _____ _____

     (Major)   (Major)   (minor)   (minor)

21. Write these cadences.

V_4^6 i   iv i^6 V   vi   I   V

22. Write these chord progressions.

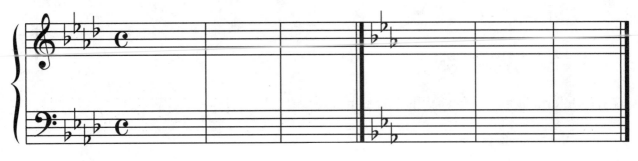

     I vi   IV ii V^7 I   i iv ii^o V^7 VI

     I IV   ii V^7 I   i iv ii^o V^7 i

23. The following example is from *Sinfonia No. 2* by J.S. Bach. Answer the questions about the music.

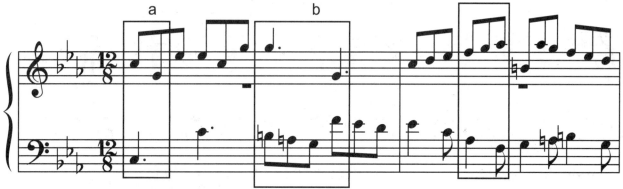

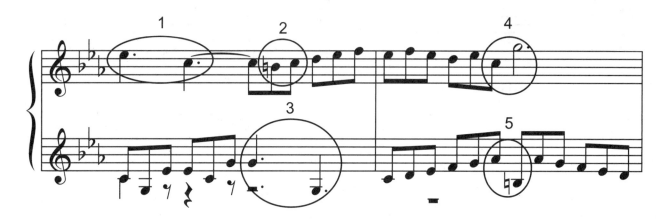

a. What is the key or tonality? _____

b. Which form of the minor scale is used in measures 1-2? _____

c. Name the circled intervals.

1. _____   2. _____   3. _____   4. _____   5. _____

d. Give the root, quality, Roman Numeral, and figured bass (inversion) for each boxed chord.

	ROOT	QUALITY	ROMAN NUMERAL AND FIGURED BASS
Chord a.	_____	_____	_____
Chord b.	_____	_____	_____
Chord c.	_____	_____	_____

24. The following example is from *Nocturne, Op. 32, No. 1,* by Chopin. Answer the questions about the music.

a. What is the key or tonality? _____

b. Name the circled intervals.

1. _____ 2. _____ 3. _____ 4. _____ 5. _____ 6. _____ 7. _____

c. Give the root, quality, Roman Numeral, and inversion of each boxed chord.

	ROOT	QUALITY	ROMAN NUMERAL AND FIGURED BASS
Chord a.	_____	_____	_____
Chord b.	_____	_____	_____
Chord c.	_____	_____	_____
Chord d.	_____	_____	_____
Chord e.	_____	_____	_____

d. What is the term for chord a? _____

e. What type of cadence is used in measures 3-4? _____

25. The following example is from *Sonata, K. 284,* by Mozart. Answer the questions about the music.

a. What is the key or tonality? _____

b. Name the circled intervals.

   1. _____ 2. _____ 3. _____ 4. _____ 5. _____

c. Give the letter name, quality, Roman Numeral, and inversion of each boxed chord.

	ROOT	QUALITY	ROMAN NUMERAL AND FIGURED BASS
Chord a.	_____	_____	_____
Chord b.	_____	_____	_____
Chord c.	_____	_____	_____
Chord d.	_____	_____	_____
Chord e.	_____	_____	_____

LESSON 11
TIME SIGNATURES

The **TIME SIGNATURE** for a composition is found at the beginning of the music, next to the key signature. The time signature is often made up of two numbers:

Sometimes, the symbol 𝐂 or 𝄵 is used instead of numbers.

𝐂 stands for $\frac{4}{4}$, or **Common Time.**

𝄵 stands for $\frac{2}{2}$, or **Alla Breve.**

The **top** number of the time signature tells **how many beats each measure contains.**

The **bottom** number tells **which type of note receives one beat.**

2 = 2 beats per measure
4 = Quarter note (♩) receives one beat

3 = 3 beats per measure
8 = Eighth note (♪) receives one beat

METER is the division of beats into groups of equal length, with accents occuring at regular rhythmic intervals. The meter is determined by the time signature, and the length of the measures. (For example, a piece in 3/4 has a triple meter, or a meter with three beats per measure.)

When the bottom number of a time signature is a "4," a quarter note (♩) receives one beat or count. The following chart shows how many beats to give these notes or rests:

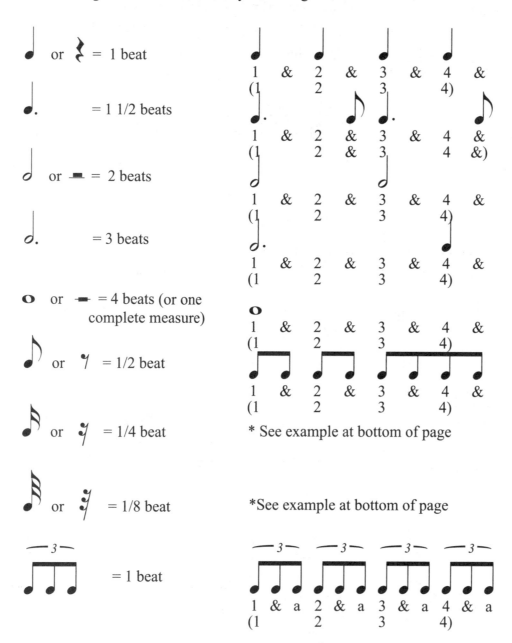

* See example at bottom of page

*See example at bottom of page

* Counting for some of the more common eighth, sixteenth, and thirty-second note patterns is shown here:

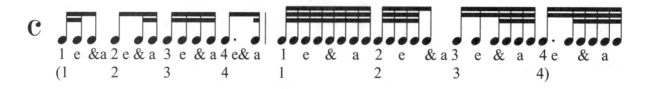

An **UPBEAT** occurs when an incomplete measure begins the piece. The last beat or beats are"borrowed" from the final measure of the piece and placed at the beginning. The beats used for the upbeat measure will be the last numbers of the time signature. The final measure will have fewer beats than normal. The first full measure begins with count number 1.

Example:

When the bottom number of a time signature is a "2," a half note (♩) receives one beat or count. The following chart shows how many beats to give these notes or rests:

90

When the bottom number of a time signature is an 8, an eighth note (♪) receives one beat.

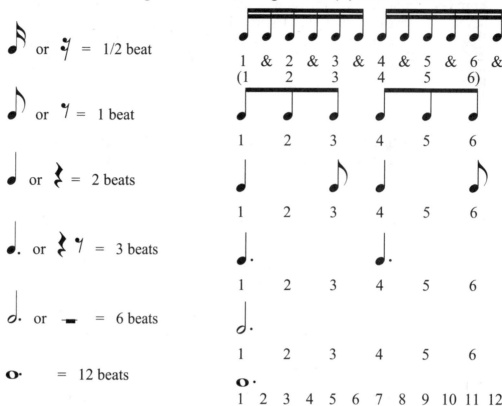

1. Fill in the blanks. (The first one is done for you.)

2 = 2 beats per measure
4 = Quarter note receives one beat or count

3 = _____
4 = _____

3 = _____
8 = _____

¢ = _____

C = _____

2 = _____
2 = _____

7 = _____
4 = _____

6 = _____
8 = _____

When a time signature has a 2 on top (2/2, 2/4, etc.), the first beat of the measure is strongest. There are two pulses per measure.

When a time signature has a 3 on top (3/8, 3/4, etc.), the first beat of the measure is strongest. There are three pulses per measure.

When a time signature has a 4 on top (4/2, 4/4, etc.), the first beat of the measure is strongest, and the third beat is slightly emphasized. There are four pulses per measure.

When a time signature has a 6 on top (6/8, 6/4, etc.), the first beat of the measure is strongest, and the fourth beat is slightly emphasized. There are **two large pulses** per measure, each containing three smaller beats.

When a time signature has a 9 on top (9/8, 9/4, etc.), the first beat of each measure is strongest, and the fourth and seventh beats are slightly emphasized. There are **three large pulses** per measure, each containing three smaller beats.

When a time signature has a 12 on top (12/8, 12/4, etc.), the first beat of each measure is strongest, and the fourth, seventh, and tenth beats are slightly emphasized. There are **four large pulses** per measure, each containing three smaller beats.

When a time signature has a 5 or 7 on top, the accented beats are irregular. Music which is in 5/4, 5/8, etc., will be divided into groups of 2 + 3 or 3 + 2. Music which is in 7/4, 7/8, etc., will be divided into groups of 4 + 3 or 3 + 4.

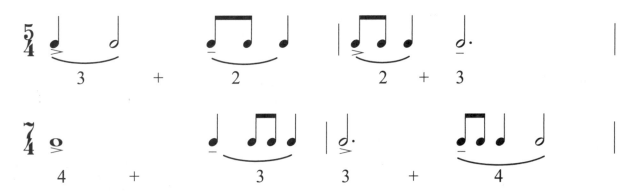

Note: The accents above are only intended to demonstrate where strong and weak beats occur within the given meter. They are not meant to imply that every strong beat receives an accent.

SYNCOPATION is a contradiction of the meter or pulse, often by changing strong and weak beats within the measure.

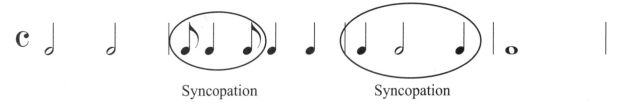

Syncopation   Syncopation

HEMIOLA occurs when the meter changes from two pulses per measure to three pulses by changing, for example, from 6/8 to 3/4 (Example A), or by the use of ties (Example B).

Example A   **Example B**

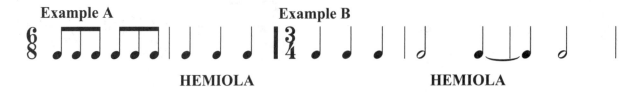

HEMIOLA   HEMIOLA

2. Write the counts for these phrases, and place accents on the strong beats. Tell how many
   pulses will be in each measure.

a. From *Invention No. 14* by J.S. Bach. _____ pulses per measure

b. From *Rhapsody, Op. 119, No. 4,* by Brahms. _____ pulses per measure

c. From *Sinfonia No. 9* by J.S. Bach. _____ pulses per measure

d. From *Sonata No. 31* by Scarlatti. _____ pulses per measure

e. From *Sonata, Op. 10, No. 1,* by Beethoven. _____ pulses per measure

f. From *Waltz, Op. 3, No. 3,* by Britten. _____ pulses per measure

g. From *Sonata, XVI:34,* by Haydn. _____ pulses per measure

h. From *Sonata, XVI:40,* by Haydn _____ pulses per measure

i. From *Sonata, XVI:42* by Haydn. _____ pulses per measure

j. From *Sonata, K. 281,* by Mozart. _____ pulses per measure

k. From *Sonata, K. 283,* by Mozart. _____ pulses per measure

l. From *Sonata, XVI:42* by Haydn. _____ pulses per measure

3. Define these terms.

a. Meter _____

b. Syncopation _____

c. Hemiola _____

LESSON 12
HOMOPHONIC AND POLYPHONIC TEXTURES

TEXTURE is the manner in which the various voices or parts of music relate to one another; how the voices are put together.

CONTRAPUNTAL or **POLYPHONIC TEXTURE** occurs when there are two or more parts which are of equal importance. The melodies are passed between the voices. This example, from *Sinfonia No. 3* by J.S. Bach, shows the use of polyphonic texture (or **Counterpoint**).

HOMOPHONIC TEXTURE occurs when there is one voice which dominates the music, while the other voice or voices serve as an accompaniment. Homophonic texture may either be **chordal*** in nature, or may have a **separate melody and accompaniment.** This example, from *Sonata, Op. 10, No. 1,* by Beethoven, shows the use of homophonic texture.

*Some theory scholars divide texture into three categories: Homophonic, polyphonic (often called contrapuntal), and chordal. Homorhythmic texture is a type of chordal texture in which each beat has a chord, such as in a four part hymn.

1. Name the texture of each example below.

a. From *Nocturne, Op. posth. 72, No. 1,* by Chopin. _____ texture

b. From *French Suite No. 1: Menuet,* by J.S. Bach. _____ texture

c. From *Rhapsody, Op. 119, No. 4,* by Brahms. _____ texture

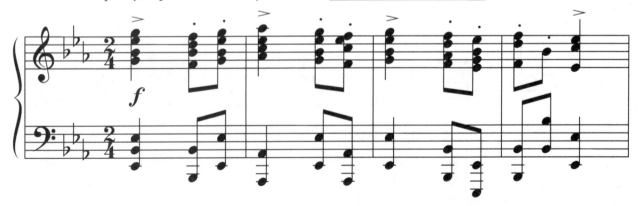

d. From *Sonata, K. 284,* by Mozart. _____ texture

e. From *Sonata No. 40* by Scarlatti. _____ texture

100

f. From *Sinfonia No. 2* by J.S. Bach. _____ texture

LESSON 13
CONTRAPUNTAL TECHNIQUES

A **MOTIVE** is a short group of notes used in a piece of music. The composer uses this motive as the main idea of the music and repeats it in many different ways.

A **THEME** is an entire phrase of music, which is the basis of the composition. (A composition may have more than one theme.)

Beethoven's *Symphony No. 5* uses this **motive:**

It is repeated, with variations, several times at the beginning of the symphony, to create the **theme:**

It would be helpful to listen to the entire first movement of Beethoven's *Symphony No. 5*, and you will hear its motive and theme used in many interesting ways.

REPETITION takes place when the motive is repeated immediately, exactly the way it was the first time it occurred, on the same note.

This example, from *Waltz, Op. 69, No. 1* by Chopin, uses repetition. The repetition is circled.

SEQUENCE occurs when the motive is repeated immediately, on a different note, usually a 2nd or 3rd higher or lower.

This example, from *French Suite No. II: Courante* by J.S. Bach, uses sequence. The sequence is circled.

IMITATION occurs when the motive is repeated immediately in another voice, such as in the bass clef following a statement of the motive in the treble clef.

This example, from *Invention No. 3* by J.S. Bach, uses imitation. The imitation is circled.

CANON occurs when the entire **theme** is repeated in another voice. The difference between imitation and canon is that imitation uses only a motive, while canon is a <u>strict copy of the entire theme.</u>

Dona Nobis Pacem shows the use of canon. Notice how the bass clef part copies the entire theme which was introduced in the treble clef.

PEDAL POINT or **ORGAN POINT** occurs when there is a sustained or repeated note, usually in the bass (although sometimes in higher voices), which stays for some time while the other voices continue to change harmonies.

This example, from *Invention No. 4* by J.S. Bach, shows the use of pedal or organ point.

AUGMENTATION is the exact doubling of the rhythmic value of the notes within a theme (for example, the quarter notes become half notes).

DIMINUTION occurs when the rhythmic values of a theme are divided in half (for example, quarter notes become eighth notes).

1. Circle the repetition, imitation, sequence, canon, pedal point, augmentation, or diminution in each example below, then write the type of compositional technique on the line above the music.

a. From *Aufschwung* by Schumann. _____

b. From *Sinfonia No. 9* by J.S. Bach. _____

c. From *Sonata, 1766,* by Haydn. _____

d. Original. _____

e. From *Sonata Hob. XVI:41,* by Haydn. _____

f. From *Sonata, Hob. XVI:41,* by Haydn. _____

g. From *Invention No. 15* by J.S. Bach. _____

h.. From *Sonata, XVI:41,* by Haydn. _____

i. From *Sonata, Op. 2, No. 1,* by Beethoven. _____

j. Original _____

k. Original. _____

l. From *Sinfonia No. 1* by J.S. Bach. _____

110

m. From *Sonata, K. 284* by Mozart. _____

n. From *Sinfonia No. 2* by J.S. Bach. _____

LESSON 14
THE FUGUE

A **FUGUE** is a style of composition in which three or more voices follow one another in an imitative manner.

The **SUBJECT** is the first voice to enter. After the entire subject is heard, the second voice enters, usually at a fifth above or below. While the second voice answers with the transposed subject, the original voice plays a **COUNTERSUBJECT** against the second voice. Similarly, the third voice enters with the subject, usually at an octave above or below the main subject, while the other two voices continue with their countersubject, and free counterpoint.

This chart shows the entrance of voices in a three-voice fugue:

First Voice	Second Voice	Third Voice
Subject		
Countersubject	Answer (Subject)	
Free Counterpoint	Countersubject	Subject

The opening section of the fugue, in which all three (or more) voices enter in their entirety, is called the **Exposition.** The fugue then continues, with **Episodes,** sections of music that do not contain the entire subject, but rather contain either new material, or motives based on the subject. These episodes are alternated with sections in which the entire subject returns, along with the countersubject. The entire subject normally returns near the end in the original key, leading up to the closing of the piece.

Terminology used in a fugue:

Exposition: The opening section, containing all voices in their entirety.

Answer: The first occurrence of the transposed subject.

Subject: The main theme of the fugue.

Countersubject: A different melody from the subject, which occurs at the same time as the subject.

Episode: A section in which the subject is not present, but instead is made up of new material, or motives based on the subject.

112

1. The sections of this fugue (BWV 847) by J.S. Bach are marked. Study them carefully.

2. Mark the sections of this fugue (BWV 856) by J.S. Bach. Include the Exposition, the subject and its answer, each subsequent entrance of the subject and countersubject, and the Episodes.

116

LESSON 15
THE DANCES OF THE BAROQUE SUITE

A **SUITE** consists of several movements. Baroque Suites contain dances, all in the same key.

The Baroque Suite has the standard scheme of:

Allemande

Courante or Corrente

Sarabande

Optional Dances (one or more): Minuet, Bouree, Gavotte, Passepied, Polonaise, Anglaise, Loure, or Air

Gigue

ALLEMANDE: A dance in moderate 4/4 time of German origin, with a short upbeat, often using short running figures that are passed through a semi-contrapuntal texture. (Example from *French Suite No. 1* by J.S. Bach.)

COURANTE: French dance in moderate 3/2 or 6/4 time, with frequent shifting from one of these to the other (hemiola). The texture is free counterpoint, with a shifting melody. (Example from *French Suite No. 2* by J.S. Bach.)

CORRENTE: Italian dance in quick triple meter, with continuous running figures, and homophonic texture. (Example from *Partita No. 1* by J.S. Bach.)

SARABANDE: A dance in slow triple meter and dignified style, often with an accented or long tone on the second beat. It probably originated in Latin America and moved to Spain as a wild dance, but when it arrived in France and England, its style became calm and dignified. (Example from *French Suite No. 2* by J.S. Bach.)

Optional Dances:

Minuet: A French country dance in 3/4 meter. (Example from *French Suite No. 1* by J.S.Bach.)

Bouree: A French dance, usually in quick duple meter with a single upbeat. (Example from *French Suite No. 5* by J.S. Bach.)

Gavotte: A French dance in moderate duple meter, with an upbeat of two quarter notes, and with phrases usually beginning and ending in the middle of the measure. (Example from *French Suite No. 5* by J.S. Bach.)

122

Passepied: A spirited dance in quick 3/8 or 6/8 meter, possibly originating in Brittany. (Example from *French Suite No. 6* by J.S. Bach.)

Polonaise: A Polish dance of stately and festive character, in moderate triple meter. It often contains measures with a short repeated rhythmic motive. (Example from *French Suite No. 6,* by J.S. Bach.)

Anglaise: A dance in fast duple meter, derived from the English country dance. (Example from *French Suite No. 3* by J.S. Bach.)

Loure: From the 16th and 17th century term for bagpipe, this dance is in moderate 6/4 time, with dotted rhythms and heavy downbeats. (Example from *French Suite No. 5* by J.S. Bach.)

Air: A song, rather than a dance, with melodic characteristics. (Example from *French Suite No. 2* by J.S. Bach.)

GIGUE: Originated from the English Jigs, the **French Gigue** is in compound duple meter (6/8, for example), contains dotted rhythms and large intervals (6ths, 7ths), and has fugal texture. The **Italian Giga** is quicker, non-fugal, and has running passages over a harmonic bass. These are less common in Baroque suites than the French Gigue. (Example of *Gigue* from *French Suite No. 6* by J.S. Bach.)

1. Match these dances with their descriptions.

_____ Courante	a. Dance in moderate 4/4 time with a short upbeat, and running figures in a semi-contrapuntal texture.
_____ Sarabande	b. French dance in 3/2 or 6/4 time, using hemiola; texture is free counterpoint with a shifting melody.
_____ Allemande	c. Minuet, Bouree, Gavotte, Passepied, Polonaise, Anglaise, Loure, Air.
_____ Corrente	d. Dance in slow triple meter and dignified style, often with an accented or long note on the second beat.
_____ Gigue	e. Italian dance in quick triple meter, with continuous running figures, and homophonic texture.
_____ Optional Dances	f. Dance in compound duple meter, with dotted rhythms and large intervals.

2. List the dances used in a Baroque Suite in their proper order.

_____

_____

_____

_____

_____

LESSON 16
SONATA FORM

A **SONATA** is a composition for piano or another instrument which has several separate sections called **movements.**

The normal scheme for the movement s of a sonata are:

Allegro: Sonata (or Sonata Allegro) form

Adagio: Binary or Ternary form, in a key different but closely related to that of the first movement (such as the dominant or relative minor).

Scherzo or Minuet: Ternary form (Scherzo and Trio or Minuet and Trio), in the same key as the first movement.

Allegro (or Presto): Rondo form or Variations, in the same key as the first movement.

This scheme is not always followed. Often times there are fewer than four movements (in which case it is usually the Scherzo/Minuet movement that is missing), or a Sonata may begin with a slow movement rather than a fast movement.

The first movement of a Sonata is usually in **Sonata Allegro** form. There are three sections:

EXPOSITION		DEVELOPMENT	RECAPITULATION	
Theme I (Tonic key)	**Theme 2** (Dominant or related key)	Motives based on Themes 1 and 2 are developed in various ways	**Theme 1** (Tonic key)	**Theme 2** (Tonic key)

Normally, the Exposition is repeated, then the Development and Recapitulation are repeated.

The first movement of *Sonata, XVI:27* by Haydn, is given below. The sections and themes (with their keys) are marked. Study this sonata.

The second movement of this sonata is a Minuet and Trio in the key of G Major (Tonic).

The third movement is a Rondo in the key of G Major (Tonic). (Music for the second and third movements are not included in this workbook.)

Theme 2 (D Major, V)

128

DEVELOPMENT
(Various keys)

RECAPITULATION
Theme 1 (G Major, I)

Theme 2 (G Major, I)

130

1. Mark the sections of this *Sonata, K. 283,* by Mozart. Include the Exposition, Development, Recapitulation, Themes 1 and 2, and their keys (letter names and Roman Numerals).

134

LESSON 17
SIGNS AND TERMS

Music often contains signs and terms other than notes and rhythms. Memorize the ones listed below.

A Tempo: Return to the original tempo (the speed at which the piece began).

 Accent: Play the note louder than the others.

Accelerando: Accelerate; gradually faster.

Adagio: Slowly.

Allargando: Broadening; gradually slower.

Allegro: Fast or quick.

Allegretto: Slighly slower than Allegro; faster than Andante.

Andante: A moderate walking tempo.

Andantino: Slightly faster than Andante. (Some composers use it to mean slower than Andante).

Animato: Animated; with spirit.

 **Appoggiatura:** Used mainly in music of the Classical Period, play the first note as half the value of the second note (other interpretations are possible):

Articulation: The manner in which notes are played - includes, but not limited to, staccato and legato.

Arpeggio: A continuous broken chord:

Atonality: No specific key or tonality.

Bitonality: The use of two different keys at the same time.

Canon: A strict form of contrapuntal writing in which each voice exactly imitates the melody of the first voice.

Cantabile: In a singing style.

Coda: An extended ending for a piece of music.

Codetta: A short Coda.

Con: With.

Con Brio: With vigor or spirit (with brilliance).

Con Fuoco: With fire or fury.

Con Moto: With motion.

Crescendo: Gradually louder.

D.C. al Fine: Go back to the beginning of the piece, and play until the word *Fine* (which means end).

Damper Pedal: Press the pedal located on the right.

Decrescendo or Diminuendo: Gradually softer.

Dolce: Sweetly.

Doloroso: Sadly; sorrowfully.

Double Flat: Two flats placed before a note, indicating to lower the note a whole step.

B double flat is played as A on the piano

Double Sharp: The symbol ✕ placed before a note, indicating to raise the note a whole step.

G double sharp is played as A on the piano.

Dynamics: Letters or symbols which tell how loudly or softly to play the music.

Enharmonic: Two different names for the same pitch, such as C♯ and D♭.

Espressivo: Expressively.

Fine: The end.

f **Forte:** Loud.

ff **Fortissimo:** Very loud.

fff **Fortississimo:** Very, very loud.

fp **Forte-piano:** Loud followed immediately by soft.

⌢ **Fermata:** Hold the note longer than its value.

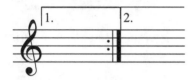 **First and Second Ending:** Play the piece with the first ending (under the 1.), then repeat the piece. The second time through, skip the first ending and play the second ending (under the 2.).

Giocoso: Merrily, with humor.

Gracioso: Gracefully.

Largo: Very slowly; "large."

 **Legato Sign (slur):** Play smoothly; connect the notes.

Leggiero: lightly, delicately.

Lento: Slowly.

m.d. *mano destra;* use the right hand.

m.s.: *mano sinistra;* use the left hand.

Marcato: Stressed, marked.

Meno: Less.

Meno mosso: Less motion; slower.

mf **Mezzo Forte:** Medium loud.

mp **Mezzo Piano:** Medium soft.

Moderato: A moderate or medium tempo.

Molto: Much; very.

 **Mordent:** An ornament in which the written note is played, followed by the note below the written note and the written note again:

138

Octave Sign (8va): Play the notes an octave higher (or lower if below the notes) than where they are written.

Opus: A word used to indicate the chronological order in which a composer's music was written.

Ostinato: A repeated pattern, such as: 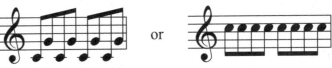 or

Parallel Major/minor: Major and minor keys with the same letter names (such as C Major and c minor).

p **Piano:** Soft.

pp **Pianissimo:** Very soft.

ppp **Pianississimo:** Very, very soft.

Pesante: Heavily.

Phrase: A musical sentence, often four measures long.

Piu: More.

Piu Mosso: More motion; faster.

Poco: Little.

Polytonality: The use of several different keys at the same time.

Presto: Very fast.

Rallentando: Gradually slower.

Relative Major and minor: Major and minor keys which have the same key signature.

Repeat Sign: Repeat the previous sections of music. Go back to the nearest repeat sign, or to the beginning of the piece if there is none.

Ritardando (*ritard., rit.,*): Slow down gradually.

Ritenuto: Immediately slower.

Robusto: Robustly, boldly.

Rubato: "Robbed time." The practice of varying the rhythm of a phrase by slowing or rushing the tempo, making up the changed time elsewhere in the phrase.

Scherzando: Playfully, jokingly.

Sempre: Always.

Senza: Without.

 Sforzando: A sudden, sharp accent.

Smorzando: Dying away.

Simile: Continue in the same style.

 **Slur:** Connect the notes; play smoothly.

Spiritoso: Spirited; with spirit.

Sostenuto: Sustained.

Sotto voce: In a low voice.

 Staccato: Play crisply or detached.

Subito: Suddenly; at once.

Syncopation: A momentary contradiction of the meter or pulse, often by changing strong and weak beats within a measure. For example:

Tempo: The speed at which to play the music.

 **Tenuto:** Hold the note for its full value. May also mean to play the note slightly louder than the others or stress the note.

Tie: Hold the second note; do not play it.

Toccata: A virtuoso piece common during the Baroque Period, written in free style with many scales and rapid passages.

Tranquillo: Tranquilly, peacefully, calmly.

Tre Corde: Release the Una Corda pedal (soft pedal; left pedal).

Trill: An ornament in which the written note is alternated with the note above:

Baroque or Classical Period: begin on the note above the written note.

Romantic Period: begin on the written note.

Trill with prefix: A trill performed with an added beginning from above or below:

Turn: An ornament in which the written note is surrounded by its upper and lower neighbors:

Una Corda: Often abbreviated U.C. in music. Press the left or soft pedal.

Vivace: Quick, lively.

Vivo: Brisk, lively.

...etto: A suffix meaning little or less than, such as Allegretto for a little slower than Allegro.

...ino: A suffix meaning little or less than, such as Andantino for a little faster than Andante.

1. Match these terms and symbols with their definitions.

_____ *ff*   a. Mezzo Piano: Medium soft

_____ *fff*   b. Pianissimo: Very soft

_____ *sfz*   c. Piano: Soft

_____ *f*   d. Fortissimo: Very loud

_____ *pp*   e. Mezzo Forte: Medium loud

_____ 8*va*   f. Symbols that indicate loud or soft

_____ Dynamics   g. Forte: Loud

_____ *mp*   h. Play one octave higher

_____ *mf*   i. Fortississimo: Very, very loud

_____ *ppp*   j. Sforzando: A sudden, sharp accent

_____ *p*   k. Pianississimo: Very, very soft

2. Match these terms and symbols with their definitions.

_____

a. Legato: Connect the notes

_____

b. Repeat sign: repeat the music

_____

c. Staccato: Crisply or detached (not connected)

_____

d. Slur: Connect the notes; play smoothly

_____

e. Fermata: Hold the note longer than its value

_____

f. First and Second Ending

_____

3. Match these terms and symbols with their definitions.

_____

a. Use the damper pedal (the pedal on the right)

_____

b. A musical sentence, often four measures long

_____ Phrase

c. Hold the note for its full value (or may mean to stress the note)

_____

d. Accent: Play the note louder than the others

_____ D. C. al Fine

e. Slow down gradually

_____ Ritardando (*rit.*)

f. Return to the original tempo (the speed with which you began the music)

_____ A Tempo

g. Go back to the beginning and play until you see the word "*Fine*"

4. Match these terms and symbols with their definitions.

_____ Allegro		a. Walking tempo
_____ Andante		b. Gradually louder
_____ Moderato		c. Slow down gradually
_____ Vivace		d. Gradually softer
_____ (decrescendo)		e. Slowly
_____ (crescendo)		f. A moderate or medium tempo
_____ Adagio		g. Quick or lively
_____ Lento		h. With brilliance
_____ Rallentando		i. Fast, quick
_____ Con Brio		j. Slowly

5. Match these terms and symbols with their definitions.

_____ *fp*		a. Sadly, sorrowfully
_____ Scherzando		b. Boldly, robustly
_____ Doloroso		c. More
_____ Opus		d. Heavily
_____ Robusto		e. Sustained
_____ Piu		f. Playfully, jokingly
_____ Pesante		g. System of classifying a composer's works chronologically
_____ Sostenuto		h. Loud, followed immediately by soft

6. Match these terms and symbols with their definitions.

_____ Andantino

_____ Con Moto

_____ Dolce

_____ [music notation]

_____ Accelerando

_____ [music notation with *tr*]

_____ Una Corda

_____ Cantabile

_____ Molto

_____ [music notation]

_____ [music notation]

_____ Codetta

_____ Poco

_____ Tre Corde

_____ Spiritoso

_____ [music notation]

_____ Coda

_____ Sempre

_____ [music notation]

a. Trill: [music notation]

b. Gradually faster

c. Trill with prefix: [music notation]

d. Use soft pedal (left pedal)

e. Slightly faster than Andante

f. Sweetly

g. With Motion

h. With Spirit

i. Little

j. Much, greatly

k. A short coda

l. Release the soft pedal (left pedal)

m. Trill with prefix: [music notation]

n. In a singing style

o. Mordent: [music notation]

p. An extended ending

q. Appoggiatura: [music notation]

r. Always

s. Turn: [music notation]

7. Match these terms and symbols with their definitions.

_____ Presto	a.	Expressively
_____ Vivo	b.	Without
_____ Espressivo	c.	Suddenly; at once
_____ Leggiero	d.	Very fast
_____ Senza	e.	Stressed; marked
_____ Marcato	f.	Brisk, lively
_____ Subito	g.	Continue in the same style
_____ Simile	h.	Lightly; delicately

8. Match these terms and symbols with their definitions.

_____ Largo	a.	Animated; with spirit
_____ Giocoso	b.	Gracefully
_____ Animato	c.	With fire
_____ Bitonality	d.	No specific key or tonality
_____ Allegretto	e.	Peacefully; calmly; tranquilly
_____ Grazioso	f.	Merrily; with humor
_____ Con Fuoco	g.	The use of two different keys at the same time
_____ Atonality	h.	Slightly slower than Allegro
_____ Polytonality	i.	Very slowly; "large"
_____ Tranquillo	j.	The use of several different keys at the same time

146

9. Match these terms and symbols with their definitions.

_____ Allargando		a. Two names for the same pitch
_____ ...etto		b. Broadening, gradually slower
_____ ...ino		c. Little
_____ Meno		d. Less motion
_____ Canon		e. Less
_____ Ritenuto		f. Strong notes on weak beats
_____ Enharmonic		g. Major and minor keys with the same key signature
_____ Parallel Major and minor		h. Immediately slower
_____ Relative Major and minor		i. Little
_____ Meno mosso		j. A strict form of contrapuntal writing in which each voice exactly imitates the melody of the first voice
_____ Piu mosso		
_____ Syncopation		k. More motion
_____ Exposition		l. Major and minor keys with the same letter names
_____ Development		m. Composition made up of separate but related pieces
_____ Recapitulation		n. The middle section of Sonata Allegro Form
_____ Fugue		o. The third section of Sonata Allegro Form
_____ Suite		p. A style of composition in which the subject (theme) is imitated by other voices
		q. The first section of Sonata Allegro Form

10. Match these terms with their definitions.

_____ Arpeggio		a. ✖ Raise the note a whole step
_____ Ostinato		b. A continuous broken chord
_____ Double Sharp		c. Fluctuation of the tempo
_____ Double Flat		d. In a low voice
_____ m.d.		e. Use left hand
_____ m.s.		f. Dying away
_____ Rubato		g. A repeated pattern
_____ Smorzando		h. Use right hand
_____ Sotto voce		i. Lower the note a whole step
_____ Toccata		j. Baroque virtuoso piece, free style, scales, rapid passages

LESSON 18
TRANSPOSITION

TRANSPOSITION occurs when a piece of music is played or written in a key that is different from the original.

For example, the first version of "Frere Jacques" below (Example A) is in the key of C Major. The second version (Example B) is in G Major. The piece has been transposed from C Major to G Major.

Notice how the intervals remain the same in both versions, and if played, the melody sounds the same, but higher in pitch.

EXAMPLE A: FRERE JACQUES in the key of C Major

EXAMPLE B: FRERE JACQUES in the key of G Major

Follow these steps when transposing a melody:

1. Determine the key of the original melody.

2. Determine the key signature of the key to which the music will be transposed.

3. Look at the first note of the original melody and determine its scale degree or its place in the scale. For example, if the original key is C Major and the melody begins on G, the starting note is the 5th.

4. The first note for the new key will be the same interval above the new tonic as the original. For example, when the new key is D Major and the starting note was a 5th above tonic, the new starting note will be A, a 5th above D.

5. Continue writing the transposition by determining each interval of the original melody and using that interval for the new melody. Add any necessary sharps or flats.

6. Check your progress by following steps 3 and 4 for any given note.

Example: Mary Had a Little Lamb, transposed from C Major to G Major.

1. Original key: C Major.

2. New key signature for G Major: F♯.

3. First note of original is E, the 3rd note of G Major

4. Starting note will be B, the 3rd note of G Major.

5. Melody moves up and down by seconds and thirds. See examples below.

MARY HAD A LITTLE LAMB in C Major

MARY HAD A LITTLE LAMB in G Major

Another way to transpose a melody is to move each note up or down the same distance. In the example of "Mary Had a Little Lamb" above, each note would be raised a Perfect 5th. The first E becomes B, the D becomes A, the C becomes G, etc.

1. Transpose this example (from *Allegro Scherzando* by Haydn) to the key of E♭ Major. Write the transposition on the blank staff below the example.

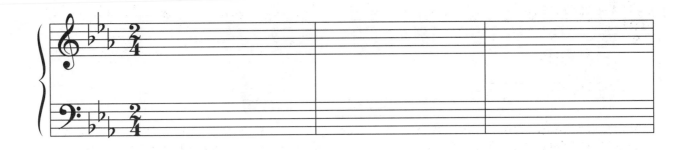

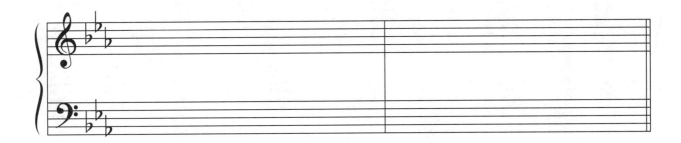

150

2. Transpose this example (from a *Polonaise* by J.S. Bach) to the key of b minor.

LESSON 19
THE FOUR PERIODS OF MUSIC HISTORY
THE BAROQUE PERIOD
CORELLI, PURCELL, AND RAMEAU

The history of music since 1600 is divided into four periods:

Baroque:	**1600-1750**
Classical:	**1750-1830**
Romantic:	**1830-1900**
Contemporary:	**1900-present**

Currently, there is not a definitive division of years for the 20th and 21st centuries. Many historians now place the Contemporary Period later, beginning after 1950 or 1960. This period can also be called "Modern" or "Post-Common Practice." Yet another division is the 20th Century (1900-1999), and the Contemporary Period (2000-Present).

Music of the **BAROQUE PERIOD** (1600-1750) is characterized by the following:

a. **Polyphonic Texture:** Two or more separate voices are interchanged to create the music. The melodies are passed between the parts, and the parts are of equal importance.

b. **Use of Ornamentation:** Composers included many trills, mordents, and other ornaments in their music. It was the performer's responsibility to know how to play the ornaments correctly. Performers could also add their own ornaments at appropriate places in the music.

c. **Improvisation:** Not only did music of the Baroque Period contain many ornaments, the performer was also free to improvise sections of the music. This not only included adding the ornaments mentioned above, but also playing **Cadenzas**, entire sections of music that the performer created, often after a cadence in the music.

Another type of improvisation in Baroque music was the use of **Figured Bass.** The performer was given an outline of the chord progression of a composition. The performer improvised using the harmonies specified by the figured bass.

Written:								6	6/4	7	
Performer Plays:	I	V	vi	iii	IV	I	IV	ii6	I6/4	V7	I
				FIGURED BASS							

d **Dance Suite:** A composition which contains many different dances, all in the same key. (See Lssson 15.)

e. Most keyboard music of the Baroque Period was written for the **harpsichord**, **clavichord**, and **organ**. The piano was not invented and perfected until late in the Baroque Period.

f. **Terraced Dynamics:** Since much of the keyboard music from the Baroque Period was written for the harpsichord, which does not have the capability of making crescendos or diminuendos, performers used terraced dynamics. This takes place when the dynamics increase or decrease by sections: *p mp mf f*, rather than gradually. (This type of dynamic contrast is most prevelant in keyboard music of the period. Other instruments, such as the violin, did create true crescendos and decrescendos during the Baroque Period.)

This example, from *Short Prelude No. 7* by J.S. Bach, shows these characteristics: Polyphonic texture and terraced dynamics.

ARCANGELO CORELLI

* Born in Italy, 1653-1713

* Violinist and composer

* Came from wealthy family; took violin lessons and performed as a young boy

* Worked as director of music to Cardinal Pamphili, and later to Cardinal Pietro Ottoboni

* Wrote several volumes of chamber music, including trio sonatas and solo violin sonatas

* Most famous work is Christmas Concerto

* Compositional style includes key changes and dissonance, which were innovative for his time

HENRY PURCELL

* Born in England, 1659-1695

* Composed songs at age eight

* Sang in boys choir at Chapel Royal

* When voice changed, worked taking care of instruments and copying music for Westminster Abby

* Eventually hired as organist for Westminster Abbey

* In 1682 became organist of Chapel Royal

* Wrote music for the coronation of James II and the funeral of Queen Mary

* Works include instrumental music, choral anthems, four operas, longer choral works with orchestra

* Music was neglected after his death until the late 1800's

JEAN PHILLIP RAMEAU

* Born in France, 1683-1764

* Son of an organist

* Went to Italy at age eighteen to study music

* Worked as organist in Avignon, Clermont, Paris, Notre Dame, and Clermont Cathedral, France

* Returned to Paris in 1722, where he remained

* Works include harpsichord works, operas, ballets, and other types of stage works, and instrumental chamber music

* Theoretical works include *Traied de l'harmonie, Nouveau systeme de musique;* was an innovator in the development of Major and minor harmony and bass movement

Some other well known Baroque composers are:

J.S. Bach, born in Germany, 1685-1750

Girolamo Frescobaldi, born in Italy, 1583-1643

G.F. Handel, born in Germany, 1685-1760

Johann Philipp Kirnberger, born in Germany, 1721-1783

Domenico Scarlatti, born in Italy, 1685-1757

Antonio Soler, born in Spain, 1729-1783

Georg Philipp Telemann, born in Germany, 1681-1767

Antonio Vivaldi, born in Italy, 1678-1741

1. Name the four periods of music history and give their dates.

2. List the five characteristics of Baroque music mentioned above, and describe each.

a. _____

_____

b. _____

_____

c. _____

_____

d. _____

_____

e. _____

_____

f. _____

_____

3. Complete the following information about each of these composers.

a. **Arcangelo Corelli**

Dates of birth and death: _____

Historical period: _____

Country of birth: _____

Positions held: _____

_____

Types of compositions: _____

_____

Compositional Style: _____

_____

b. **Henry Purcell**

Dates of birth and death: _____

Historical period: _____

Country of birth: _____

Positions held: _____

_____

Types of works: _____

_____

c. Jean Phillip Rameau

Dates of birth and death: _____

Historical period: _____

Country of birth: _____

Positions held: _____

_____

Types of compositions: _____

_____

Theoretical works: _____

4. Name eight other Baroque composers, their places of birth, and their dates of birth and death.

_____   _____   _____

_____   _____   _____

_____   _____   _____

_____   _____   _____

_____   _____   _____

_____   _____   _____

_____   _____   _____

_____   _____   _____

LESSON 20
THE CLASSICAL PERIOD
BEETHOVEN, HAYDN, AND MOZART

The **<u>CLASSICAL PERIOD</u>** of music took place from approximately 1750-1830. Music from the Classical Period includes the following characteristics:

a. **<u>Homophonic Texture:</u>** Much of the music of the Classical Period has an obvious melody, with accompaniment.

b. **<u>Cadence points usually obvious:</u>** Quite often, the harmonic structure of Classical music is clear, and the cadences are obvious, both harmonically and by the use of rests at the ends of sections.

c. **<u>Alberti Bass:</u>** A common type of accompaniment for the left hand part of piano music from the Classical Period is Alberti Bass, a repeated pattern in this style:

ALBERTI BASS

d. **<u>Sonata and Sonatina forms</u>** developed. See Lesson 16 for a detailed explanation of Sonata Form.

This example, from *Sonatina, Op. 36, No. 3* by Clementi, shows these characteristics: Homophonic texture, clear melody and harmony, and use of rests.

LUDWIG VAN BEETHOVEN

* Born in Bonn, Germany, 1770-1827

* Went to Vienna in 1790 to work as a professional pianist and teacher

* Know in his performances for improvising

* Studied with Haydn

* Made his living as a professional composer (via commissions, dedications to royalty, etc.)

* Much of his music was influenced by events in the French Revolution

* Lost his hearing completely, yet continued composing

* Works include string quartets, piano concertos, piano sonatas, symphonies, works for solo instruments, piano trios

* Helped bridge the gap between the Classical Period and the Romantic Period with his style

FRANZ JOSEF HAYDN

* Born in Austria, 1732-1809

* Studied at the Vienna Choir School

* Was dismissed from the school when he played a practical joke on a fellow student

* Began his career as a teacher and professional singer

* Was later hired to a permanent position as music director to Prince Esterhazy

* Did some travelling to London to compose and direct

* Works include piano sonatas, operas, string quartets, over 100 symphonies, giving him the title "Father of the Symphony" or "Papa Haydn"

* Developed the standard four-momement format for symphonies, and Sonata Allegro form

WOLFGANG AMADEUS MOZART

* Born in Austria, 1756-1791

* Child prodigy; performed and travelled throughout Europe with his father Leopold and sister Nanerl

* Began improvising and composing before age five

* Travelled extensively throughout Europe as a young man, composing and performing

* Worked as music director for the Archbishop of Salzburg, but conflicts with his employer caused this position to cease

* Went to Vienna to live and work as a professional composer and teacher

* Lived much of his life in poverty

* Works include piano sonatas, piano concertos, operas, symphonies, sonatas and concertos for other instruments, a Requiem for choir and orchestra

Other composers of the Classical period include:

Muzio Clementi, born in Italy, 1752-1832

Carl Czerny, born in Austria, 1791-1857

Anton Diabelli, born in Austria, 1781-1858

Frederich Kuhlau, born in Germany, 1786-1832

1. List the four characteristics of music from the Classical Period mentioned above, and describe each.

a. _____

_____

_____

b. _____

_____

_____

c. _____

_____

_____

d. _____

_____

_____

2. Complete the following information about each of these composers.

a. **Ludwig van Beethoven**

Dates of birth and death: _____

Historical period: _____

Country of birth: _____

Types of compositions: _____

_____

Music influenced by: _____

_____

Studied with: _____

b. **Franz Josef Haydn**

Dates of birth and death: _____

Historical period: _____

Country of birth: _____

Education: _____

Musical form which he developed: _____

Positions held: _____

_____

Types of works: _____

_____

c. **Wolfgang Amadeus Mozart**

Dates of birth and death: _____

Historical period: _____

Country of birth: _____

Childhood: _____

Types of compositions: _____

_____

Positions held: _____

_____

3. Name four other Classical composers, their places of birth, and their dates of birth and death.

_____   _____   _____

_____   _____   _____

_____   _____   _____

_____   _____   _____

LESSON 21
THE ROMANTIC PERIOD
BRAHMS, LISZT, AND TCHAIKOVSKY

The **<u>ROMANTIC PERIOD</u>** was from approximately 1830-1900. Music of the Romantic Period is the most popular of the four periods of music history. Some characteristics of this music are:

a. **<u>Programme Music:</u>** Much of the music of the Romantic period was written about things, people, places, or feelings. The titles in music of the period reflect the mood of the piece (such as *Curious Story* by Heller, *Blindman's Buff* by Schumann, or *Valse Melancolique* by Rebikoff).

b. **<u>Harmonies more complicated:</u>** Composers began to add more colorful notes to their chords, using more chromaticism, and straying from the tonal scale.

c. **<u>Lyric melodies:</u>** Many of the melodies in music of the Romantic period are lovely, singing melodies that have become favorites among music lovers.

d. **<u>Rhythms more complicated:</u>** Music of the Romantic period contains many syncopated rhythms, complicated sixteenth note patterns, dotted rhythms, triplets, cross rhythms (two against three), etc.

This example, from *Reaper's Song* by Schumann, shows these characteristics: A descriptive title, more complex chords, more complicated rhythms, lyric melody.

JOHANNES BRAHMS

* Born in Germany, 1833-1897

* Son of a bass player

* Supported himself as a teenager by playing piano in taverns

* Toured Europe with the violinist Remenyi in 1853

* After the tour, visited Liszt and Schumann, who helped launch his career

* After Schumann's death, remained close friends with his wife Clara

* Worked as musical director at a small court in Detmold, and later as conductor of the Singakademie in Vienna

* After the success of his German Requiem in 1868, he made a living as a professional composer and performer

* Works include two piano concertos, sonatas, piano quartets and quintets, the Requiem, other choral works, symphonies, short piano pieces, clarinet sonatas

* Enjoyed fame during his lifetime, and was offered honorary degrees from Cambridge and Breslau

FRANZ LISZT

* Born in Hungary, 1811-1886

* Son of an amateur musician

* As a boy, received financial assistance based on talent which allowed him to study with Czerny and Salieri

* Child prodigy; travelled and performed

* As an adult, had a reputation as the greatest pianist ever, and extremely popular

* In 1848 became Kappelmeister Extraordinary in Weimar

* Music inspired by his homeland (Hungary)

* Works include many piano pieces: sonatas, Hungarian Rhapsodies, Consolations, ballades, polonaises, Transcendental Etudes, and more. Also wrote piano concertos, symphonic poems, songs, transcriptions of works by Berlioz, Beethoven, Schubert, and others, choral works, including oratorios

PETER ILYICH TCHAIKOVSKY

* Born in Russia, 1840-1893

* Attended the St. Petersburg School of Jurisprudence from ages 10-19

* Studied composition with Anton Rubinstein

* Taught at Moscow Conservatory from 1866-1878

* Wrote textbooks, including *Guide to the Practical Study of Harmony*

* Works include operas, symphonic poems, ballets (*Swan Lake* and *The Nutcracker* being the most famous), piano concertos, symphonies, violin concerto

* Influenced by the folk music with which he was raised

Other Romantic composers include:

Frederick Chopin, born in Poland, 1810-1849

Antonin Dvorak, born in Prague, 1841-1904

John Field, born in Ireland, 1782-1837

Edvard Grieg, born in Norway, 1843-1907

Stephen Heller, born in Hungary, 1813-1888

Felix Bartholdy-Mendelssohn, born in Germany, 1809-1847

Franz Schubert, born in Austria, 1797-1828

Robert Schumann, born in Germany, 1810-1856

1. List the four characteristics of music from the Romantic Period mentioned above, and describe each.

a. _____

_____

_____

b. _____

_____

_____

c. _____

_____

_____

d. _____

_____

_____

2. Complete the following information about each of these composers.

a. **Johannes Brahms**

Dates of birth and death: _____

Historical Period: _____

Country of birth: _____

Works:_____

_____

_____

Composers with whom associated: _____

_____

b. **Franz Liszt**

Dates of birth and death: _____

Historical Period: _____

Country of birth: _____

Childhood: _____

_____

Positions held: _____

_____

Types of compositions: _____

_____

_____

Inspired by: _____

c. **Peter Ilyich Tchaikovsky**

Dates of birth and death: _____

Historical Period: _____

Country of birth: _____

Education: _____

Positions held: _____

_____

Types of compositions: _____

_____

_____

Other contributions to music: _____

_____

Influenced by: _____

3. Name eight other Romantic composers, their places of birth, and their dates of birth and death.

_____   _____   _____

_____   _____   _____

_____   _____   _____

_____   _____   _____

_____   _____   _____

_____   _____   _____

_____   _____   _____

LESSON 22
IMPRESSIONISM IN MUSIC
DEBUSSY, RAVEL, GRIFFES

IMPRESSIONISM is sometimes used to describe music of a few late 19th and early 20th century composers, particularly Debussy and Ravel. The term is actually borrowed from that used to describe the paintings of Monet, Degas, and Renoir, whose images are blurred, creating an impression rather than a clear picture.

"Impressionistic" music contains unclear tonalities, non-metric rhythms, and tends to flow, in musically blurred images. Compsers used whole tone scales, pentatonic scales, parallel chords, augmented triads, and ostinato figures.

This example, from the Prelude *Voiles* by Debussy shows use of the whole tone scale, parallel thirds, is musically "blurred," and contains an ostinato figure.

CLAUDE DEBUSSY

* Born in France, 1862-1918

* Received no formal music training until 1871 when he entered the Paris Conservatory

* Studied composition with Guiraud

* Won the Prix de Rome in 1884 with his cantata *L'enfant prodigue*

* Made his living as a professional composer and conductor

* Works include piano preludes and etudes, opera, orchestral works, *Children's Corner* suite for piano

* Style of music is freer than conventional Romantic style, with emphasis on color and timber rather than form and harmony

MAURICE RAVEL

* Born in France, 1875-1937

* Raised in Paris; attended Paris Conservatory

* His well known work *Bolero,* for orchestra, uses a single melody which is repeated over and over, building from a single instrument to the full orchestra in a crescendo of color

* Other works include *Pavane for a Dead Princess* for piano (later scored for orchestra), *Miroirs* for piano, *Scheherazade* for orchestra, ballet *Daphnes and Chloe*

* Well known for his beautiful orchestrations of his own and others' works

CHARLES TOMLINSON GRIFFES

* Born in U.S.A., 1884-1920

* Studied piano with Mary Selna Broughton, who financed his later studies in Berlin at the Stern Conservatory

* Returned to the U.S. in 1907, and taught at the Hackley School in Tarrytown, New York

* Early compositions are more structured; later works show the influences of the Impressionistic movement

* Also influenced by traditional Japanese songs

* Works include songs, chamber music, stage works, a piano sonata, several short pieces for piano

1. Name some of the characteristics of Impressionistic music.

_____

_____

_____

_____

2. Complete the following information about each of these composers.

a. **Claude Debussy**

Dates of birth and death: _____

Historical Period: _____

Country of birth: _____

Education: _____

Made living as: _____

_____

Types of compositions: _____

_____

_____

172

b. **Maurice Ravel**

Dates of birth and death: _____

Historical Period: _____

Country of birth: _____

Education: _____

Types of compositions: _____

_____

_____

Besides compositions, known for: _____

c. **Charles Tomlinson Griffes**

Dates of birth and death: _____

Historical Period: _____

Country of birth: _____

Education: _____

Positions held: _____

_____

Types of compositions: _____

_____

_____

Influenced by: _____

LESSON 23
THE CONTEMPORARY PERIOD
COPLAND, IVES, GERSHWIN

Many changes have taken place in the way music sounds during the **Contemporary Period (1900-present).**

a. **Major and minor tonalities avoided**, with non-tonal (not in Major or minor keys) harmonies being used.

b. **Quartal Harmony:** The use of 4ths to make up chords, rather than thirds.

QUARTAL HARMONY

c. **Bitonality:** The use of two different keys at the same time.

BITONALITY

d. **Polytonality:** The use of many different keys at the same time.

POLYTONALITY

174

e. **Atonality:** No specific key used.

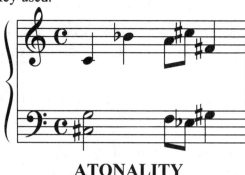

ATONALITY

f. **Irregular and changing meters:** Composers often use uncommon time signatures such as 5/4 or 7/4, or change the time signature during the course of the music (complex meter).

g. **Polyphonic texture:** This texture is often used, with the harmonies becoming the result of the entangling of the melodic lines.

h. **Neo-Classic writing:** Composers often write Sonatas, Sonatinas, or other forms which were common during the Classical Period.

i. **Serial or Twelve-Tone Music:** A style of writing in which the twelve tones of the chromatic scale are arranged in a fixed style, or series. The entire piece will then be based on the intervals of the series.

The **Prime** is the original series, usually presented first in the composition.

The **Inversion** is created by inverting all the intervals of the prime (for example, P4 up becomes P4 down).

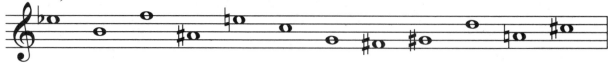

The **Retrograde** is created by reversing the prime.

The **Retrograde Inversion** is created by inverting the intervals of the retrograde.

This example, from *Evening in the Country* by Bartok, shows these characteristics: polyphonic texture, changing (complex) meter, avoidance of Major and minor tonalities.

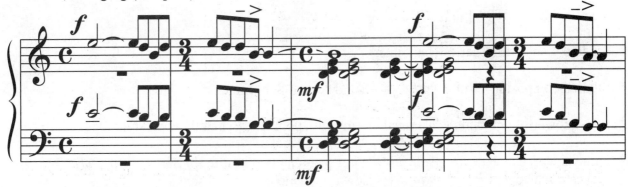

AARON COPLAND

* Born in U.S.A., 1900-1990

* Began piano study at age thirteen

* Taught at New School for Social Research in New York from 1927-1937

* Taught composition at Tanglewood (1940-1965)

* Early works show use of neo-classic style combined with jazz elements

* Later works show a distinctively American style, influenced by folk music

* Famous works include *El Salon Mexico,* the ballets *Billy the Kid, Rodeo,* and *Appalachian Spring,* a Piano Concerto, and varied works for solo instruments and piano

* Wrote two books, *The New Music,* and *Music and Imagination*

CHARLES IVES

* Born in U.S.A., 1874-1954

* Taught the fundamentals of music by his father

* Studied with Horatio Parker at Yale

* Made his living as an insurance agent

* Style was highly innovative, using bitonality, atonality, use of two different and clashing meters at once, quartertones

* Works include many songs, several of which use well known tunes or hymns arranged in 20th Century style; he also wrote piano sonatas, orchestral works, and chamber music

GEORGE GERSHWIN

* Born in U.S.A., 1898-1937

* Studied piano with Charles Hambitzer

* Studied composition with Henry Cowell and Joseph Schillinger

* Best known for combining "classical" forms with popular (especially jazz) style

* Famous works include *Rhapsody in Blue* for piano and orchestra, *An American in Paris* for orchestra, the opera *Porgy and Bess;* also wrote piano pieces and songs

Other Contemporary composers include:

Bela Bartok, born in Hungary, 1881-1945

Benjamin Britten, born in England, 1913-1976

Norman Della-Joio, born in U.S.A., 1913-

Dmitri Kabalevsky, born in Russia, 1904-1987

Francis Poulenc, born in France, 1899-1963

Sergei Prokofiev, born in Russia, 1891-1953

Dmiti Shostakovich, born in Russia, 1906-1975

Igor Stravinsky, born in Russia, 1882-1971

1. List the nine characterisitcs of music from the Contemporary Period mentioned above, and describe each.

a. _____

_____

_____

b. _____

_____

_____

c. _____

_____

_____

d. _____

_____

_____

e. _____

_____

_____

f. _____

_____

_____

g. _____

_____

_____

h. _____

_____

_____

i. _____

_____

_____

2. Complete the following information about each of these composers.

a. **Aaron Copland**

Dates of birth and death: _____

Historical Period: _____

Country of birth: _____

Education: _____

Positions held: _____

Style: _____

Compositions: _____

Books: _____

b. **Charles Ives**

Dates of birth and death: _____

Historical Period: _____

Country of birth: _____

Education: _____

Style of writing: _____

_____

Works: _____

_____

_____

c. **George Gershwin**

Dates of birth and death: _____

Historical Period: _____

Country of birth: _____

Education: _____

Style: _____

_____

Works: _____

_____

3. Name eight other Contemporary composers, their places of birth, and their dates of birth and death.

_____	_____	_____
_____	_____	_____
_____	_____	_____
_____	_____	_____
_____	_____	_____
_____	_____	_____
_____	_____	_____
_____	_____	_____

REVIEW
LESSONS 11-23

1. Write the counts for these phrases, place accents on the strong beats, and tell the number of main pulses per measure.

a. From *Invention No. 15* by J.S. Bach. _____ main pulses per measure

b. From *Sonata, Hob. XVI:40,* by Haydn. _____ main pulses per measure

c. From *Nocturne, Op. 55, No. 2,* by Chopin. _____ main pulses per measure

2. Define these terms.

a. Atonality _____

b. Exposition _____

c. Fugue _____

d. Enharmonic _____

e. Parallel Major and minor _____

f. Polytonality _____

g. Suite _____

h. ritenuto _____

i. scherzando _____

j. Syncopation _____

k. Hemiola _____

l. smorzando _____

m. Toccata _____

n. sotto voce _____

o. Rubato _____

3. Circle the compositional technique used in each of these examples (repetition, sequence, imitation, pedal point, canon, augmentation, or diminution), and write the type of technique on the line above the music.

a. From *Sonata, XVI:34*, by Haydn. _____

b. From *Sonata, XVI:34*, by Haydn. _____

c. From *Sonata, XVI:42*, by Haydn. _____

4. Name the texture of each of the following examples.

a. From *Invention No. 15* by J.S. Bach.

182

b. From *Sonata, Hob. XVI:34,* by Haydn. _____

5. Name the three sections of Sonata Allegro form, and how the themes are used within those sections.

_____   _____

_____   _____

_____   _____

6. Each of the following terms belongs either with the Dance Suite or the Fugue. Match the terminology.

a. Fugue   **b. Dance Suite**

_____ Subject   _____ Passapied   _____ Bouree

_____ Courante   _____ Loure   _____ Exposition

_____ Corrente   _____ Gavotte   _____ Minuet

_____ Polonaise   _____ Countersubject   _____ Gigue

_____ Sarabande   _____ Allemande   _____ Anglaise

_____ Air   _____ Episode

7. Match the following occurences in music history with the appropriate period.

    a. Baroque   b. Classical   c. Romantic   d. Impressionsim   e. Contemporary

_____ Sonata form developed

_____ Use of ornamentation

_____ Irregular and changing meters

_____ Homophonic texture predominates

_____ Lyric melodies

_____ Programme music

_____ Polyphonic texture in which harmonies are determined by the combinations of each individual line

_____ Whole tone and pentatonic scales

_____ Dance Suites

_____ Serial or Twelve Tone music

_____ Harmonic structure and cadence points clearly defined

_____ Atonality, Bitonality, and Polytonality

_____ Colorful harmonies (within Major and minor tonalities)

_____ Polyphonic texture (within Major and minor tonalities)

_____ Alberti bass

8. Give the historical period, dates, and three important facts about the life of each composer listed below.

Ludwig van Beethoven:

184

Franz Liszt:

Claude Debussy:

Charles Ives:

Jean-Phillipe Rameau:

Arcangelo Corelli:

Wolfgang Amadeus Mozart:

Maurice Ravel:

Peter Ilyich Tchaikovsky:

Franz Josef Haydn:

Aaron Copland:

186

Henry Purcell:

George Gershwin:

Charles Griffes:

Johannes Brahms:

9. Transpose this music, from *Ballade* by Burgmuller, to the key of f# minor.

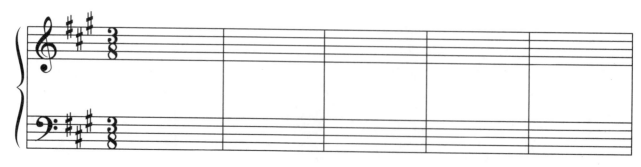

Score: _____   **REVIEW TEST**   Perfect Score: 100
Passing Score: 70

1. Name these intervals. (8 points)

Melodic Intervals   Harmonic Intervals

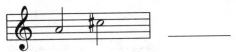 _____    _____

 _____   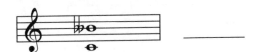 _____

 _____    _____

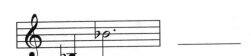 _____   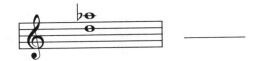 _____

2. Give the name of the Major and minor key for each of the following key signatures. (The first one is given.) (8 points)

	Major Key	**Minor Key**
	F	d
	_____	_____
	_____	_____
	_____	_____
	_____	_____

188

3. Add the necessary accidentals to complete these melodies in the keys given. (5 points)

a. E Major

b. g melodic minor

c. f♯ natural minor

d. Whole Tone

e. b harmonic minor

4. Determine the time signature for each of the following rhythms. (4 points)

a. _____

b. _____

c. _____

d. _____

5. Give the quality of each seventh chord. (Use the terms Dominant 7th, Major 7th, minor 7th, diminished 7th, and half diminished 7th.) (6 points)

_____ _____ _____ _____ _____ _____

6. Give the name of the ehharmonic equivalent for each of the following notes. (4 points)

Eb _____   B _____   C# _____   Fb _____

7. Match these terms with their definitions. (10 points)

_____ Serial Music

_____ Modulation

_____ Development

_____ Fugue

_____ Subject

_____ Recapitulation

_____ Atonality

_____ Episode

_____ Allemande

_____ Parallel Major and minor

a. The main theme of a fugue

b. The third section of Sonata Allegro form

c. A style of writing in which several voices imitate each other

d. Twelve tone music

e. Change of key

f. A section of a fugue in which the entire subject is not heard

g. A dance in moderate 4/4 time with a short upbeat

h. Major and minor keys with the same letter name

i. The second section of Sonata Allegro form

j. No specific key or tonality

190

8. Match the historical period with the technique. (5 points)

_____ Baroque   a. Whole Tone Scales

_____ Classical   b. Sonata Form

_____ Romantic   c. Polytonality

_____ Impressionism   d. Use of ornamentation

_____ Contemporary   e. Lyric melodies

9. The following example is from *Rondo No. 3* by Bartok. Answer the questions about the music. (12 points)

Piu lento

1. Give the letter names and qualities of the basic harmonies for measures 1-6.

Measure 1: _____ Measure 2: _____ Measure 3: _____

Measure 4: _____ Measure 5: _____ Measure 6: _____

2. What is the meaning of *piu lento*? _____

3. Is the key of this example well defined? _____

4. Give the Italian name and English meaning for the symbol *pp*. _____ _____

5. Name two other composers from Bartok's historical period. _____ _____

10. The following example is from *Sinfonia No. 7* by J.S. Bach. Answer the questions about the music. (12 points)

a. What is the key or tonality? _____

b. How many main pulses are in each measure? _____

c. What is the texture? _____

d. Name the circled intervals.

   1. _____ 2. _____ 3. _____ 4. _____

e. Give the letter name and quality of the chord on beat 2 of measure 3. _____

f. Give the letter name and quality of the chord on beat 3 of measure 4. _____

g. Which period of music history does J.S. Bach represent? _____

h. Name two other composers from this same period. _____ _____

11. The following example is from *Sonata, Hob. XVI:52* by Haydn. Answer the questions about the music. (14 points)

a. What is the key or tonality? _____

b. What compositional technique is used in measures 2-3? _____

c. What compositional technique is used in measures 3-4? _____

d. How many main pulses are in each measure? _____

e. Name the three sections of Sonata Allegro Form.

_____ _____ _____

f. Give the letter name and quality of the seventh chord on beat 1 of measure 3. _____

g. Give the Roman Numerals (Figured Bass) for measure 1, beats 2 and 3. _____ of _____

What is the name for this type of chord movement? _____ _____

h. Which period of music does Haydn represent? _____

i. Name two other composers from this same period. _____ _____

12. The following example is from *Intermezzo, Op. 118, No. 1,* by Brahms. Answer the questions about the music. (12 points)

a. What is the key or tonality? _____

b. Give the letter name and quality of the seventh chord on beat 1 of measure 1. _____

c. Give the letter name and quality of the seventh chord on beat 1 of measure 6. _____

d. Name the circled intervals. 1. _____ 2. _____ 3. _____ 4. _____

e. How many main pulses are in each measure? _____

f. Which period of music does Brahms represent? _____

g. Name two other composers from this same period. _____ _____

REFERENCES

Apel, Willi. *Harvard Dictionary of Music, Second Edition.* Cambridge, Massachussetts: Belknap Press of Harvard University Press, 1972.

Arnold, Denis, ed. *The New Oxford Companion to Music, Volumes 1 and 2.* New York: Oxford University Press, 1983.

Music Teachers' Association of California. *Certificate of Merit Piano Syllabus.* San Francisco: Music Teachers' Association of California, 1992.

Music Teachers' Association of California. *Certificate of Merit Piano Syllabus.* Ontario, Canada: Frederick Harris Music Co., Limited, 1997.

Music Teachers' Association of California. *Certificate of Merit Piano Syllabus.* San Francisco: Music Teachers' Association of California, 2007.

Russell, John. *A History of Music for Young People.* Toronto, Canada: Clark, Irwin & Company Limited, 1965.

Sadie, Stanley, ed. *The New Grove Dictionary of Music and Musicians.* Washington, D.C.: Grove's Dictionaries of Music Inc., 1980.

BASICS OF KEYBOARD THEORY

Workbooks by Julie McIntosh Johnson
Computer Activities by Nancy Plourde

NAME _____

ADDRESS _____

CITY_____ STATE_____ ZIP_____

PHONE _____ E-MAIL_____

QTY	ITEM	COST	TOTAL
	PREPARATORY LEVEL	9.50	
	LEVEL 1	9.50	
	LEVEL 2	9.50	
	LEVEL 3	9.95	
	LEVEL 4	9.95	
	LEVEL 5	10.50	
	LEVEL 6	10.50	
	LEVEL 7	10.95	
	LEVEL 8	11.95	
	LEVEL 9	12.95	
	Level 10 (Advanced)	12.50	
	ANSWER BOOK	11.95	
	COMPUTER ACTIVITIES LEVELS PREP-2, Mac/PC	49.95	
	COMPUTER ACTIVITIES LEVELS 3-4, Mac/PC	39.95	
	COMPUTER ACTIVITIES LEVELS 5-6, PC Only	49.95	

Shipping:
1-5 Books.........$5.00
6-10 Books.......$6.00
11 or more........$7.00

Sub-Total	
Calif. Residents: Sales Tax	
Shipping	
TOTAL	

Make checks payable to:

J. Johnson Music Publications

5062 Siesta Lane

Yorba Linda, CA 92886

714-961-0257   www.bktmusic.com   info@bktmusic.com